A T

Remember:
He Chose you!
Ta
John 15:16

A Teacher's Prayer

© 2011 by Tammy Mentzer Brown
St. Clair Publications

ISBN **978-1-935786-32-0**

Printed in the United States of America by
St. Clair Publications
P. O. Box 726
Mc Minnville, TN 37111-0726

http://stclairpublications.com

Cover Design by Kent Hesselbein
© 2012 KGH Design Studio
http://www.kghdesignstudio.com/services.html

A Teacher's Prayer

Tammy Mentzer Brown

Edited by Stan St. Clair

A Teacher's Prayer

A Teacher's Prayer

Dedication

Frances Kuzmicki Lokey
Born October 20, 1921

There are so many people that have sometimes inadvertently and many times deliberately impacted my life. For me, the power of hope and trust would not be possible without each and every one of you: Patrick, Anthony and Lauren Brown for teaching me love and trust in family; Frances Lokey, Earl Hill, Kelvin Cunningham, Becky Davis, Van Blankenship, Neil Thorne, and Santanu Borah for being great teachers and friends; Sharon Span Moore, John Morris, Mama Flo, Joni Huth, Patricia Cochran, Annie Beck, Rana Cowan, Ms. Carol, Ms. Catherine, Ms. Betty, Ms. Nichols and Tiffany Satterwhite Quarfordt who believed in me and caused me to believe in myself; and with special appreciation and love to the staff and children from the Presbyterian Home for Children — each of you helped to change my life in such a blessed way!

A Teacher's Prayer

And in Loving Memory of Myron Uptain - who forever will be in my heart. Thank you for the advice along the way!

Special thanks to my sister-in-law, Rachel Brown of Rachel Brown Photography for the family picture on the back cover. With great appreciation and thanksgiving to my editor Stan St. Clair and to Kent Hesselbein for being patient and helping me come up with just the right cover.

A Teacher's Prayer

Prologue

Proverbs 22:6 (NKJV)
Train up a child in the way he should go,
And when he is old he will not depart from it.

As a child, I realized that just because someone was older, by no means was that person grown up. Early on in life, I was forced to learn self preservation and the true meaning of opportunity—this wasn't always a positive statement. I am confident there are hundreds of thousands of children, each day in the United States, who learn these same basic concepts of survival. The sad part is that a lot of times they learn it at home. This is ironic, when we spend so much time blaming the schools and their friends. Rarely do we reflect on the environment of home life. How often do we look at the verbal or physical abuse which takes place in the home?

According to the CWIG (Child Welfare Human Gateway) of the US Department of Health and Human Services over 3 million reports of child abuse are documented each year in the United States, with some reports containing multiple children. Children in the United States of America are suffering from an "epidemic of abuse and neglect."[i] Startling statistics on the factsheets found on our government's welfare website show the following:

- *A report of child abuse is made every ten seconds*
- **More than **five children die every day** as a result of child abuse.*
- *Approximately 80% of children that die from abuse are under the age of 4.*
- *It is estimated that between 50-60% of child fatalities due to maltreatment are **not recorded as such on death certificates.***

A Teacher's Prayer

• More than 90% of juvenile sexual abuse victims know their perpetrator in some way.
• Child abuse occurs at every socioeconomic level, across ethnic and cultural lines, within all religions and at all levels of education.
• About 30% of abused and neglected children **will later abuse their own children,** *continuing the horrible cycle of abuse.*[ii]

This book is a touching story about the journey and courage of an abused young girl and those who made it different, whether they knew it at the time or not. Running away at age fifteen, it was not too late to reach her and provide her an out from being another statistic.

Currently there are studies being done to explore why some children emerge unscathed from long-term abuse, even with similar conditions as those who do not. The resilience of the character of the child has become a focal point including their ability to cope and thrive following that experience. Such characteristics like, "… optimism, self-esteem, intelligence, creativity, humor, and independence, as well as the acceptance of peers and positive individual influences such as teachers, mentors, and role models." [iii] Whatever research shows, I know that each of these traits are embraced and shared by believers in a God who created man.

This book is dedicated to all of the teachers—at school and in churches—who go beyond the classroom setting, and get on a bended knee or their heart folds just a little when they peer into the eyes of one of our lost children!

---

[1] http://www.childhelp.org/pages/statistics
[ii] http://www.childwelfare.gov/pubs/factsheets/long_term_consequences.cfm
[iii] http://www.childhelp.org/pages/statistics

A Teacher's Prayer

Chapter 1 – My Daddy

We were a fairly representative American family, I suppose, clinging to the hopes, dreams and desires sought out in the early 1970s. Our family lived in a comfortable two story home on the outskirts of Cedar Rapids, Iowa. There was one thing, however, which was somewhat different from far too many families. We had so much that I don't recall ever wanting for anything. Our father worked for Iowa Steel and Iron Works, while Mother stayed at home to raise my brother, Sam Jr., and me. Sam was fifteen months my senior and a typical ornery older brother, both bossy and mean behind the scenes. But he was also my playmate and my best friend.

In our backyard was a large greenhouse that Daddy had built to house his enormous cacti collection. My maternal great-grandfather, William "Buck" Holland, exposed Dad to this rare hobby. Green thumbs ran strictly between our parents as Dad handled his cacti and Mom her multiple flower beds. To this day, I can take her a plant that I have been unsuccessful at growing and by the time I come back for the next visit, it is not only alive but flourishing and more beautiful than it ever was in my care.

Weeknights were quite the routine in our home. Dad would return from work in the late evening, covered in a mix of sweat and dirt accumulated after a long day at the mill. The first thing he would do is give our Mother a big kiss. Mother always prepared a warm, inviting dinner. She was happy to cater to his every need. Sam Jr. and I were usually found peeping around the corner of the kitchen cabinet, because we were just as excited to see Dad. However we knew our time came after he bathed.

More times than not, as we watched, our giggles would give us away and earn us a head rub upon his exiting the room. To us, there was just something amusing about watching our parents kiss on the lips. Maybe it was our age or maybe it was the happiness that Daddy brought into our home when he returned each night.

"Hey, Dee," he said, leaning up to kiss Momma.

"Sam," she acknowledged while wiping off her hands then extending her arms out to receive her hug. "How was your day?"

"It was okay," he said with an awry smile.

"Okay?" she inquired. Sometimes we would hear about work. Other times he was quiet.

"Well...it was good. Johnnie got hurt on the mill, but thank goodness nothing too serious."

"Sam! What is it this time?" Momma asked

"Dee, don't get all worked up," he assured her. "It was just a valve that didn't shut right and the steam flew out and scorched his arm a bit. It's fine, honey."

"I don't like that place. I just have a bad feeling," she quipped.

"Diana, it pays our bills and does so very well, I might add," he boasted. "Besides, you know we keep talking to upper management about getting the safety devices put on. It's just at this time the cost is more than they're willing to put into it."

"At what cost?" Momma asked. "Too much has happened there in the past few years."

"Now look...quit worrying your pretty little self," he said, tilting her chin towards him and kissing her. "I am home, aren't I? In one piece...right?"

A moment of silence pursued as Momma nestled her head into his shoulder.

"Diana, right?" he asked.

My father, who was a God-fearing man, always reminded Momma that we would be safe, that God is always in control.

"Yes, Sam, you are home in one piece."

Another moment of silence filled the room then a bit of horseplay followed. "Hey," she called out after him as he affectionately popped her with the dish towel before tossing it on the counter and heading to the shower, "you are meaner than anyone I know. You're right, nothing to worry about at all."

As he sauntered around the corner, he yelled back from down the hallway, "Someone has to keep you in order. Heck, with the way you're talking, you'd think I didn't come home tonight."

Dad shut the door to the bathroom and Momma finished dinner.

Every night, following his shower, Dad would call Sam Jr. and me into the living room for our nightly bout of wrestling.

"Sam, Tammy, where are you?" he called while laying flat on the floor. "Where are my monkeys?"

Sam, giggling, and me screaming—as any four-year-old filled with excitement—we bounded into the living room and as usual, plopped onto our father. Dad, of course was hungry, but each night prior to his meal, this was our ritual and we would wrestle until he wore us out and was able to tuck us into bed.

Most mornings we awoke to Momma's cooking. Each day, my brother and I started with the anticipation of watching Superfriends, a cartoon in the early to mid seventies. It's hard to imagine today's kids getting excited about watching the cartoon on our television, because it was an awkwardly large piece of furniture. No LED, LCD, or plasma, but simply powered by a picture tube with unlimited access to all four channels. Flat screens were not an option in that day, nor the clarity in colors, but we knew no difference as long as the super heroes came blazing across the screen — and they did. Watching our cartoons, lazing around in our pajamas, we would devour our breakfast, usually washing it down with a glass of milk.

Again, as each morning before he left for work, mother asked him, "Sam Mentzer, you come home to us safely tonight?" She demanded only one answer from him.

Again, as always, he replied, "I promise, Dee. I love you." And with that, they kissed and he walked out the door. Every single work day the same conversation would replay. In my four-and-half-year-old mind the question seemed goofy to me and quite the disturbance to my super heroes show. I knew he would come home safely, so why didn't she? He did every day, so it just didn't make sense that Momma kept asking him that dumb question. At some point one would think the ritual would make it an irrelevant thought, especially to a four year old, yet is bothered me the same each time.

The routines of June 30, 1977 are seared into my memory in more detail than most other mornings. The morning was hotter than normal. My brother, Sam Jr., and I had gone out to play on our swing. I could feel the piercing heat on my skin and my lungs when I would take in a breath. Despite the heat, we loved our backyard. It

12

was our own little park with a simple metal set that supported a couple of swings and a double-seated glider that swayed back and forth. Unfortunately, on that day, between the heat and the swing, I learned that cheese, in the amounts that I had ingested, did not sit well on the stomach.

"Stay in and cool off," Momma replied as she began cleaning me up. I was *so* upset, as I thought she was making us come in because I got sick. But this was game night and she needed our help cleaning. Oddly enough, helping Momma clean for game night was a pleasure and I soon forgot the recent troubles of the back yard.

"Hey Aunt Sue, what are you doing here?" Sam Jr. asked upon entering the kitchen from the backyard.

"Hey kids," Aunt Sue replied as she patted our heads, "just helping your Momma."

We knew card playing and beer were in order when Aunt Sue came over. Seeing Aunt Sue made cleaning the house okay because it meant our home would be full of laughter, music and food. I remember how Aunt Sue's silky brown hair flowed around her shoulders. Daddy always said Aunt Sue was a small-built woman but had a big personality, covering a feisty temper. She wasn't really our aunt. She and Uncle Ron were our parent's best friends and they were the ring leaders of game night; whereas Momma and Daddy simply opened their home for it.

"Sue, can you grab the *Cheesewhiz* out of the cabinet?" Diana asked.

"Sure Dee. Here you go."

"Thanks."

A Teacher's Prayer

"Oh my…so, explain to me what you are doing… that looks disgusting." Aunt Sue said, smirking at Mom.

"It's new. Let the jury stay out until you try it. We had these over at Nita's house. You haven't had anything until you've bitten into one of these." Momma held the toothpick with a baby dill pickle wrapped by a blanket of thin ham and cheese spread in the air, rotating for Aunt Sue to observe.

"Maybe I should just take your word for it," Sue added, then glanced over at me and made a frowning face. I laughed in spite of them both. They could be so silly at times.

"Seriously, Sue, come on. Try it," Momma added. The two of them pushed that snack back and forth until Aunt Sue surely would give in, because my momma never gave up at anything, as I would later learn.

With that, Sue reached over and picked me up, shoving me out towards my mother. "Open up Tammy. Mommy has something she wants to feed you."

I burst out laughing so hard that Aunt Sue nearly dropped me. Momma then handed me the snack which I welcomingly swallowed before being moved into the other room.

It was mid afternoon. Momma and Sue were laughing about something when the phone rang. The details are so vivid. The house was crystal clean as the sun shone in through the windows. The temperature had dropped from that morning, as we were accustomed to in Iowa. Days start out hot then taper off as evening begins to push in. Momma had the front door open, allowing the breeze to flow in through the screen door. That only enhanced the smell of ammonia on the floors and provided a crisp, clean aroma combined with the *Pledge* that dusted the whole living area.

Momma made her way to the phone, laughing at something Sue or Sam or I had done. "Hello?" she answered and then there was a dull moment of silence. "This is Mrs. Mentzer?" She questioned instead of answered. For that split second the call seemed normal, but immediately was replaced by an eerie sound that slashed the silence. "Dear God." Momma cried out, "Sam!"

I wasn't quite five yet, but in two weeks I would officially be old enough for kindergarten, so my mind was definitely working overtime attempting to grasp the sounds and comments coming from my mother. I wanted to listen more, but I wasn't used to the tone she was speaking with. Her voice was so stricken with panic that I didn't know how to react. In no time, Sam Jr. rushed to her side, throwing his tiny arms firmly around her knees. He feverishly waited for her next response. I continued watching, trying to make sense of it all.

Silence struck the house and by this time Aunt Sue was standing at Momma's side. Her body was very tense, as she leaned against the wall for support and continued to listen to the caller.

After a few minutes of complete silence, she let out a large wail, "No, no, please say it isn't true!" she begged of the person on the other end of the line.

"You're a liar, you're a liar! It's not true!"

Momma began randomly screaming out slurs. Sue tried to embrace Momma as she kept demanding Sue to say that they were lying. Momma let the phone drop from her hand with a thud to the wall. She first looked at Sam

15

Jr., then me. Finally moving her stare to Sue, with tears pouring down her face and in a blank stare, no color in her face, she softly spoke as if all of her breath had been sucked out of her, "Sam is dead...we have to get to the hospital!"

Aunt Sue braced Momma as she grabbed the receiver. Momma hung it up on the base and pushed her away.

Momma petitioned, "Please God, say it isn't true," as she cried out with weeping that could shatter hearts in two. My brother ran down the hall towards his bedroom crying, "I want my Daddy!"

Aunt Sue grabbed Momma and pulled her into her arms, while squatting on the floor to join her, with tears of her own and prayers to God echoing those of Momma's.

As I stood there watching and listening I became agitated. Surprisingly the sobbing and screaming were all emotions I understood. I knew what dead meant. Superman had to rescue many victims from the evil witch so she wouldn't kill them. I thought I had a concept of death; therefore I questioned why I didn't cry. Yet, I didn't really understand. I did know, however, that I wasn't crying. I was well aware of that fact. I found myself unable to do anything but stand there and try to figure it all out.

Some time had passed before Momma walked over to me to give me a tight hug. She squeezed me so hard that I almost lost my breath.

"Tammy, your Daddy loved you so much," she said while sobbing. "I am so sorry, Honey. He loved you so much and he will miss you so much. Do you hear me? He loved you, baby. He loved you." She said this again and again before releasing me, with each syllable barely being spoken without some sort of deep breath or slight tear attached to it. She eventually let go of me and left the room to go check on Sam. In the meanwhile, Aunt Sue picked up the phone to call Uncle Ron and asked him to meet us at Memorial Hospital. When we arrived at the hospital, the doctor and his nurse entered the lobby to speak to us.

I remember these words to this day, "Mrs. Mentzer," the doctor called out. Momma stood up to meet him. "I'm sorry to have to tell you, but your husband was at work and...." The doctor began explaining that Daddy was at work when a massive steel counter weight being held up by a crane shifted, heading straight for my dad. The guys who worked with him tried yelling at him to warn him of the danger. The ones close to him even turned off their machines to get his attention. There was just too much noise, so Dad couldn't hear them. It happened so quickly. When the weight shifted Daddy was pinned between it and the flask, which was filled with sand and metal, killing him instantly. Uncle Ron had to brace Mom as he told her of the event. I then watched my Mom, white as a ghost, walk off down a long, cold, empty hall, with Uncle Ron and the doctor, to say her final goodbye to my daddy. I wasn't used to all of the confusion in my four- year-old mind. Dad not there, Momma acting weird and so much sadness. We were a happy family, it was game night. We needed to get home and eat and play cards, but instead, Sam and I stayed with Aunt Sue in the lobby.

It was late that night when we got back home. At least that is how I recall it. Who knows how long we had actually been there? I remember that night I lay in my bed next to one of the front windows of the house and looked up to the sky. Usually there was a sense of peace staring into that huge star-lit sky; but on that night there was a sense of coldness. I waited in anticipation for Dad's arrival. I didn't understand. I knew sometimes he came home late from work and I could never fully fall asleep until he gave me that kiss goodnight and said to me, "I love you, Pumpkin."

Beneath the beautiful city lights of Cedar Rapids, I waited for my Daddy. I remember that after a while of staring out the window, my heart started aching. It started hurting in a way I had never felt. From the depth of my heart to the pit of my stomach as a heavy knot was tying them together. I tried to ignore it as I kept looking out at the sky. It looked awfully lonely on that particular night.

Where is the moon? Mr. Moon, where are you? I thought to myself, getting frustrated that nothing was making sense. I imagine that not being able to find the moon to focus on, as I sometimes could with Daddy pointing it out, must have made the sky seem emptier than usual. Even the few planes that flew by couldn't bring a sense of activity to it. *Where is my daddy? Too many planes I have seen tonight. I don't like those lights! Sky, why aren't you any darker? Go away lights — I don't like you! Where is my daddy?*

"Daddy...Daddy...Daddy," I began to cry out louder and louder until finally I remembered, *"Sam is dead!"* Daddy isn't coming home anymore. No more good night kisses for his little angel, his little pumpkin. I cried. At that moment, I finally understood death.

"Oh, Daddy, I love you, please come home?" I begged out loud. With a very broken heart, I fell asleep. It was the first time, but definitely not the last, that I felt pain this deep. Yes, the pain I felt on this night hurt so much worse than any stubbed toe or bee sting. Nobody could kiss it and make it go away.

Proverbs 3:5 (NKJV)
Trust in the Lord with all your heart,
And lean not on your own understanding.

Chapter 2 – Finding Heart in Dixie

Momma took the settlement from Iowa Steel and Iron Works and moved us to Dunnavant, Alabama. With her parents down that way and no other family to fully rely on, she knew she would need help raising us two children and decided it best to leave Iowa, and the home she and Daddy had made for us. She set out to find a place close to her parents and chose to build on some land that she bought from them. Momma wasn't just choosing to run away from what had happened, she was running to shelter for us. She had been in tough spots before and knew how to survive, and as with her first bout with fate years earlier, she exercised a valuable lesson: leaning on family.

"Let's go Sam & Tammy. No looking back kids, your Dad is not here anymore," Momma stated as she escorted us out the front door the day of the move. Grandpa had flown to Iowa, picked up the moving van and met us on the door stoop of Uncle Jimmy's, where we stayed while our house was being built in Alabama, to take us to our new home. Hugs were passed and while I know he was happy to provide his home to our family, as was his family so gracious in receiving us, it was hard having two families under the same roof: one with three kids, a wife and a farm to tend to and another that consisted of a deeply-mourning widow and her two children. On the day we left I remember Sam Jr. walking to the car with his head hanging low and hands tucked away in his pant pockets. He didn't say a word for quite some time on the trip down. I clung to my teddy and

20

hopped up into the U Haul pressing my face against the truck door window, looking back at Uncle Jimmy's truck and farm. I knew things were changing and I was ready for that change — or so I thought. Driving down the interstate, I watched rows of corn for countless miles, having no clue of the differences that my window view in passing through each state would bring. While we left the house in Cedar Rapids shortly after Dad died, we would return to that city again in a few years; we just didn't know it at the time.

"Look, Sam!" I pointed with excitement upon seeing the numerous trees lining the roads. "Oh, look!" I exclaimed again to a non-responsive brother while admiring the overgrown, humungous leaves that swarmed the hillsides sporadically. Everything was so green, alive and beautiful to behold for a girl who had only, outside of the city, seen miles and miles of cornfields, large land lots possessed by pig sties and silos stacked randomly along any given drive. To be in The Heart of Dixie seemed quite the irony when my heart seemed to be just what was missing. In Alabama, no one could've foretold the 180 degree turn our family's lives would take.

The biggest joy that would come from moving would be getting to know my grandmother better. I loved to sit and listen to her string together her yarns about my mother and father. I would begin to request stories and explanations of behaviors, even more as I got older, and these stories helped to shape my opinions and acceptance of my family today. Grandma loved to talk about Momma and her younger days. To tattle somewhat on the handful Momma was, but I also believe she was laying a foundation of understanding for me as I matured.

A Teacher's Prayer

"Tammy, your mother was quite the looker and she knew it." She would say, "She was a beautiful, wild-spirited teenager with the only accountability to her life being herself. Yeah, she was a handful!" Grandma would state.

Grandma was a creature of habit. Our conversations always were unwinding for her as she talked of Momma's fiery spirit. As she spoke, Grandma would deeply inhale a smoke of cigarette only to release after holding her breath and telling some small part of one of Diana's stories. Between the puffs and sips of *Tab* cola I learned what events had shaped my momma to be the woman she was.

My mother was also born in Iowa, but to a father who didn't want a girl in the family, it just wouldn't do for his farm. So Grandma made a choice and chose Momma over the farm and her husband. I'm not sure at what point she met the man whom I would grow up to know as my grandfather, but he would be the one to raise my mother. Unfortunately, as many stories go, too much horseplay at home by a man who wasn't her natural father, drove my mother out to find different freedoms in the world.

Whether true or not I can not attest, but Grandma told me of all kinds of stories of when Momma rebelled. Like the time she ran away from home at age fourteen to join the circus with a thirty-eight-year old man, or the time she ran away to join Hell's Angels — although I understood it to be an unsuccessful attempt. Then there was the absolute factual one: when my mother met a guy who swept her off her feet. He was quite the James Dean: good-looking, savvy and genuinely risqué. Mom was attracted to him, saw him as an easy way out and ran away to marry him, much to my grandparents' disapproval. Her man loved to hot rod and one day, some time after she gave birth to Jim, their first son, he and mom were out driving around when he succeeded in getting the car airborne. Seatbelts did not carry enough value at the time to have a law, let alone be required in all vehicles, so there was no way to prevent what would happen.

Racing through the air, adrenaline pumping and Diana screaming, they whaled to the ground only to have Momma's head hit the dashboard with blunt force. They didn't realize it at the time, but would soon discover the affects of such a stunt. One night while babysitting, Momma complained of an increasingly painful headache. Shortly thereafter, Grandma and Grandpa were called to the hospital to meet her. She was found in an unresponsive coma that lasted six months. The doctors stated that she had suffered an aneurism and that they feared she would remain in a vegetable state for the remainder of her uncertain life. Grandpa, however, determined there was too much fight within her to give in to such a prediction.

I recall Grandmother stating, "Tammy I know a God that is far superior to any human understanding. Our prayers and the connection to physical healing are not to be limited by man. We have to set our expectations for far more in life."

Grandma shared with me that eventually, this woman (my mother, Diana) who the experts said would never walk, talk, eat by herself or have children again, miraculously learned to do all. Unfortunately she would lose her first son, as his Dad divorced her while she was in the coma and took away all custodial rights to their only child. My momma and my oldest brother would be separated for many years, but in her heart he would always stay, and they did meet again in this lifetime.

I can still remember the many times Grandma would laugh, telling her proud momma story about her only girl beating the odds, and how blessed we are to have doctors in this world, but to remember they don't know it all. Grandma couldn't explain why Daddy died and wasn't healed or some miraculous intervention didn't occur. She questioned this many times, herself. What she could do though was assure me that death is emanate and while we do not know our day or time, when it is time, it does come and hopefully our lives have been lived as a witness and testimony to our Lord and Savior so that we will be reunited with those loved ones again for eternity. We don't know all the answers. Many times we can look back and reflect on what happened to us and see how miraculously God moved through those situations. I came to the realization that at some point we have to stop playing God, trying to conclude each answer that will perfectly fit within a box that we define as 'human acceptance.' I can rest on the simple understanding that He chose to love me and allows me to lean on Him for faith in His plans for my life. With this assurance comes a strength that is equally unexplainable by man.

In conversation, my grandmother would also clarify that while my father's death could've destroyed Diana, this strength and love would also suffice as to why my momma would survive losing the best person that ever came into her life. Grandma was mostly right but she didn't know everything that was going on at home. Momma indeed had been destroyed and the hopes we had for starting over in Alabama did not amount to much. To this day, I believe my mother did the best with what she had but I also believe she was limited in her capabilities.

What Grandma didn't need to tell me was the obvious, which I could observe. My mother was crippled due to partial paralysis of her right leg and she wasn't able to drive us anywhere: to get groceries, to pay bills, to go on vacations, or to go to church. What Grandma did tell me is that Momma had some psychological issues too, and my dad, balanced her in a way they had never seen before and feared they would never see again. Unfortunately, she was right.

The move to Alabama that summer was the first of many moves with Momma and Sam Jr. The home we built wasn't the fanciest in the neighborhood, not made of brick and it definitely wasn't the home we'd had in Iowa, but it provided for our needs. The rooms were small: big enough for a bed and dresser, with little area to walk around and almost no room for extra things such as toys, but we each had our own room, and that was nice. It was a cottage-style house covered with yellow siding and the front yard was surrounded by a chain-link fence and gravel road which linked our home to our grandparents'. On the back of our home was a long, covered porch which extended out over the hill, providing a picturesque view of a creek. The hill leading down to the creek was very steep and covered with kudzu (remember the big gorgeous green leaves that sporadically covered the hillsides upon my first entering the state). The kudzu crowded the sides of the banks in such a manner that the only thing brave enough to go through it were the snakes that lived there. Because it was an absolutely gorgeous Leprechaun green color in the summer, it provided a blind eye to the true depth of the hillside.

Dunnavant Creek served as a community play-ground for the neighborhood children. It was a small, clear creek, which ran very slowly most of the year. When rainy days would provide a swifter current to the creek, my friends and I would lay on the floor of the cold, shallow and rocky waterbed, challenging the water to rush our arms down by our sides. The feeling of the water pushing our arms against us gave us thrills of sorts. An enjoyment that was only intensified as we lay there staring up into a bridge of tree branches which arched over the creek…those simple childhood pleasures that most adults never take the time to feel, but children get an absolute delight from.

Some days we crossed the creek and continued on across Dunnavant Mountain in search of other forms of adventures. We would investigate any crack and crevice we could find. Our hopes were that it might somehow be turned into a mysterious cave or cavern, possibly hiding the treasure of an arrowhead not uncovered in previous expeditions. To this day, I don't remember ever finding an arrowhead, Tommy-hawk or any pottery. While the treasures hidden on these hills were few and far between, the perils were numerous. We had to avoid the snakes, fight the spiders and watch out for the old mountain man that lived just on the other side of the bridge which crossed over the creek.

The man was real. I had seen him on numerous occasions. He had the appearance of a hairy and dirty man who would send chills down my spine and fill my head with scary stories that weren't there in the moments before I'd see him. He was probably not as old as he looked and our stories over time made him even older than this. He lived off the land, growing his own food and using the creek as his water source for drinking and bathing. Our perception of the mountain man held fast for years, until the day he saved my brother's life after he'd been bitten by a water moccasin. In the blink of an eye, the mountain man had forever transformed himself from the dirty, long-bearded, loner on the mountain to the child-hood hero of our neighborhood, Mr. Kirby. I would meet Mr. Kirby again, later in life at my grandmother's funeral and he laughed stating that it was simply a childhood tale, as he had no recollection of it. It turns out that the creek was only utilized while he built his home which was equipped with all the modern amenities of running water and electricity.

During the next ten years there were many lone days, including those in Dunnavant. In my younger days, I would pack a peanut butter and jelly sandwich along with some water and head over to Grandpa's bait shop to dig red worms out from under his rabbit bins. I would then spend the whole day fishing on the creek, crouching on the bridge with my cane pole, allowing the sun to beat down upon my head while waiting for that perfect catch. Sweat would roll down my back and I actually welcomed it. Perspiration wasn't a product of activity or exertion, but of simply spending a mid-July day outside in Alabama. Whether it was fishing, laying in the stream of water that barely touched my ears, or anticipating the direction of jolt that my next crawdad victim would take, I loved living near the creek. I smile remembering times in my pre-teen days, with my friends riding bikes out on woodland trails, playing backyard football with the neighborhood guys or spending the night over at a friend's house.

Times spent with friends and solitary moments on the banks of the creek, became my escape from the harsh reality of home. When I was outside with the creek flowing, the birds singing and the frogs and crickets making their own melodious sounds, I was able to find release in my surroundings. I found a peace of sorts in the serenity of nature.

Jeremiah 6:16 (NKJV)
Thus says the LORD; Stand in the ways and see,
And ask for the old paths, where the good way is and walk in it;
Then you will find rest for your souls.

A Teacher's Prayer

Chapter 3 – Elementary Years

I attended kindergarten in Iowa before moving to Alabama. I was five or six when we left my Uncle Jimmy's home and moved to Dunnavant. Chelsea Elementary, a county school, became the place where I would attend first through third grades. I recall starting this school and being fascinated with the cubbies, the giant chalkboard, and how everything around seemed larger than life and exciting. These were years of innocence. A time when children, as a rule, haven't learned to recognize when things are wrong and mostly see goodness in everybody. No place for discrimination among peers: what color you are, how much money you have, what you wear to school, what size of house you live in, what your parents drive or where you go to church. Instead, what you find are a lot of young eager minds learning how to be away from home. Enjoying meeting new people and making friends their size with similar interests.

While this concept of acceptance was ideal, it was a hard one for me to grasp. From second grade up, I would continuously find myself in trouble. Could it have been that the abuse in my home started around this time, or could it have been just the age instead? I really don't know how to answer that. What I do know is at Chelsea Elementary I was constantly in the principal's office — mostly getting a paddling for: fighting on the playground, saying bad words out loud to my teacher or other children, playing pranks on the teacher (including placing unwanted bugs in areas like her desk drawer or chair), and stealing. The list is probably longer but I have elected to forget some of the messier details.

A Teacher's Prayer

Maybe it was an attention-getter, but I tend to lean towards my revenge for always getting caught. There were several teachers throughout my elementary and middle school years that would become of vital importance to my emotional growth. And specifically, there is one who would come to be an unknown foundation for me, supporting me in such a way to keep me held up over the years ahead and all the while without my knowledge. She was my second grade teacher, a grandmother figure, and in particular, one I remember as being very, very strict. Not that I didn't give her plenty of opportunities to use both characteristics.

"Tammy Mentzer!" Mrs. Lokey very loudly summoned me. Immediately I wanted to hide behind everyone standing in line in front of me.

"Ma'am?" I asked, realizing there was nowhere to hide.

"Young lady…" she warned as she approached. Staring up at her, I knew she wasn't happy. Surely she didn't see that last thing I did, yet she had to…*Oh no!* I thought to myself, *here I go again.*

In no time Mrs. Lokey swooped past her desk, scooping up a ruler and stood before me expecting my submission.

"Hold out your right hand, Tammy," she instructed.

I held up my right hand, barely extending it past my waist.

"Young lady, turn it over and stick your palm up."

Whack went the sound of the discipline onto me. "Now, I expect I will not see you kissing another boy in my classroom. Do we agree?"

"Yes, ma'am," I said, while trying not to cry but allowing some whimpering, more like slipping breath, to seep out.

"Go to the back of the line. You will be last at lunch today."

I turned as a whipped pup, mostly embarrassed that everyone in the class now knew. Funny, I don't recall who I kissed or what, if anything, happened to him, but I do remember learning to be more selective of when I made bad decisions from that point on. Teachers and I just didn't seem to get along. At the time they seemed too nosey and had an uncanny knack at being around when I least wanted them to. For the rest of that year, Mrs. Lokey would provide me a hug on occasion and would keep me sitting close to her desk. I thought it was because she was keeping her eyes on me and wanted me to know that. The only thing Mrs. Lokey, or any other teachers knew, was what I did in their classroom. And as soon as school was out, I went back home to no accountability. It would come to pass that many teachers would try to reach out to me as well, but I just didn't understand that at the time. It is quite possible that they saw something sad in my eyes or maybe even physical marks that provided warning signs, but none of them ever directly asked me. Maybe they knew there wouldn't have been an answer.

My second grade year would also include a happening in my life that would build an unshakable foundation for my future. In warmer weather, if we were short on groceries, Momma would walk with us to the local gas station and country market down the road from our home. There we could get basics like detergent, milk

31

and eggs and charge it to an account to be held until the next month when she drew her Social Security check.

One summer morning, we were walking through a narrow isle with bread and jams heading towards the checkout when a man approached Momma and called her by name. This was not entirely unusual in our small mountain community, as Momma was known by most.

"Ms. Mentzer, I'm Tom," he offered as he extended out his hand to shake hers, "How do you do this fine day?"

"Okay. Can I help you?" she responded, only barely accepting his shake.

"Well, yes, ma'am. Our church is having Vacation Bible School next week and I just wanted to see if your kids might like to come?"

Momma let out a weird laugh, almost as if she were mocking him and answered, "Sir, I'm sorry, but you must not see too well. I can't drive." She propped her hand on a shelf beside us and stuck her leg out for him to observe the metal brace that fitted up to just below her knee.

"I see," he said, not surprised in the least.

"So your answer is no," Momma abruptly added.

"But, Ms. Mentzer, pardon me for asking again. We have a church van that will be running and we'd be more than happy to come by and pick them up," he continued. Granted, he didn't know my momma like I did or he would have understood her *no* and walked away. If I could have disappeared at the time I would've. But all I could do was try to hide behind Momma with embarrassment at the anticipation of her obvious response.

A Teacher's Prayer

Who do you think you are? She said NO, now go away!
I said to him in my head. I was already embarrassed about
what Momma was surely to say and how she would act.
We had been in the store before when strangers approached Momma to ask some odd question of her.
Momma stood tall, releasing the shelf that propped her.
Here it comes, I thought to myself. *Just go away, sir. Please,
you don't know.* He didn't read my thoughts and I wasn't
about to speak up.

"Mrs. Mentzer, please consider it. We'll even feed
them a meal while they're with us."

"Tom...you said?"

"Yes, ma'am."

"So...you can pick them up? Can you bring them
home?"

"Yes, ma'am," he replied.

"And you say you'll feed them too?"

"Oh, yes, ma'am. Every day."

"Well, they ain't got no church clothes." She threw
out another opposition. *What's church clothes,* I thought to
myself.

"Ms. Mentzer, they can come in whatever they
have. It's summer and most kids will be in shorts and t-
shirts." He kept answering Momma calmly and quickly as
if he had anticipated every question she would ask.
Momma turned and looked down at me hiding behind her
back.

"Tammy, get out here. This man is invitin' you to
Vacation Bible School. Do you wantta go?"

I had no clue what Vacation Bible School was, but I
did know that I'd do anything to get out of my house. He
looked like a nice enough man and we never got to go

anywhere except school, unless we could walk or ride our bikes to it. I was so excited that Momma was actually asking me, but I knew not to show it.

"Yeah, please, can I go, Momma?" I asked very timidly, figuring she might be putting on, just to be polite.

"Alright, Tom. You can pick up both Sammy and Tammy. What time do I have to have them ready?"

"We get started at 9:00 A.M., and I should have them back home around 12:30 P.M.," he replied. The rest of the conversation became a blur due to my excitement. I was positive something would happen to get in the way. He would forget us and not pick us up or Momma would change her mind and not let us go. My pessimism was proven wrong.

On the van ride, which was no more than two miles from our home, we sang VBS songs on the way to and from the church each day. At first, none of the words were familiar to me, yet it didn't take long to know them all by heart: *Deep and Wide, Father Abraham* and so many more. Walking in I encountered kids I attended school with, all there for the same reason. There were many adults too. My memories of VBS revolved around very excited and happy people. The entire week, there was dancing and singing and telling stories about this man named Jesus. I just took it all in. Especially the *Kool-Aid* and big sixty cookies, they served at snack everyday, with crème-filled centers. They were delicious and I didn't get this very often at home. I couldn't recall ever being around such happy people since my father had passed.

Each day that week started with a gathering including a pledge to the American Flag, the Christian flag and an anthem of Onward Christian Soldiers. We would dismiss from the gathering and separate off into age appropriate classes which included: crafts, games and stories. My VBS teacher was unique in that I knew her. It turned out to be Mrs. Carol, my school bus driver. Reflecting back, I know in my heart that God placed her there that year to teach my class. Due to my home life trust was not an affordable trait, so to hear a new concept from someone who was affiliated with the school system wasn't coincidental. I trusted my teachers and I trusted Mrs. Carol, unfortunately I did not trust my home or the company kept there.

Each day Mrs. Carol told a different story and all of them were about the same man, Jesus. All week I sat in her class and listened to the stories, but it was the story she told on that last day which made a deeper connection than any other. She asked us to imagine one person loving us so much, that no matter what we did, no matter how bad we might have thought we had been, He was willing to die so that our sins would be forgiven because He loved us that much. When Mrs. Carol told me that Jesus had died on the cross for me because He loved me that much, I wept. Just imagine a seven year old child needing to really hear the words, "You are loved no matter what." I was seven years old and had not heard and believed "love" since before my father's death. Why? Easy, I was bad, stayed in trouble all the time and equally so bad things happened to me. My mother didn't even protect me and while I didn't know it at the time, she just wasn't capable. Love had become a foreign concept — only a word. But Mrs. Carol told me that Jesus did love me and not just in word but also in action. For me to be loved so unconditionally was something I longed for. Even having

A Teacher's Prayer

Mom tell me that my Dad loved me no matter what, wasn't as real as those words to me on that day. Did my mother love me? Yes, but filling the emptiness she was suffering crowded out the affection and attention she was able to give to us kids.

On the last day of VBS, I gave my heart to the Lord, through tears and repentance, embraced by my school bus driver and others. After that, there wasn't a day I didn't want to go to church. To think it all started with one man extending an invitation to a widow's children. Such a simple act of love and answered call he felt on his heart and I will be forever grateful. That year I learned the song lyrics and a few scriptures, like John 3:16 that would tuck away in my heart as hope to cling to in some of the most desperate times of my life that were yet to come.

My third grade year was not any easier than the second. Home life was getting worse. Momma had several different boyfriends who would come and go. She began a horrible pattern in her life that would drain our financial security as well as the definition of "safety" in our home. With each new boyfriend, she squandered away Dad's settlement by trying to buy love through the purchase of cars and clothes so that they could supposedly go find a job. When the prospect of a new job was not important she would buy expensive tools to fix up our house that was already showing signs of disrepair and neglect. New tools, cars, and clothes would be bought each time a boyfriend would enter with promises of income and service. We would watch this predictable misuse of our mother reoccur time and again over the upcoming eight years.

A Teacher's Prayer

Third grade was the year I remember the bar visits beginning. The nights were empty without her there. That year I began staying up late waiting on her to come home, remembering what it was like when Dad didn't come home. It was hard to sleep when Momma had spent so much time preaching at us, teaching us that she could also be taken away from us in a blink of an eye. The thought of losing her too was simply unbearable.

Not only did I learn to play the parental role by waiting up on my mother but by age seven, I was cooking and cleaning the house from toilets to laundry, and by age eight I was mowing the grass. As for school, Momma tried to be interested. She seemed to care about whether or not I had homework but mostly she cared about whether or not I did my chores. I was always thrilled when Momma would actually try to help me with my spelling words. It was about the only schoolwork she felt capable of helping me with and I think she enjoyed helping me as much as I enjoyed it. She would call out the word (to the best of her ability to pronounce it) and I would get to spell it back. A very simple act, but I loved to spell because of it.

On occasion she tried to help with math...as long as there were flash cards. If the subject became too complicated she would become very disinterested or pass the task on to someone else. My third grade year, learning multiplication tables became one of the hardest lessons I would undertake. Momma had allowed a boyfriend of hers to come live with us for a while. On one particular night, he offered to help me with my homework. When he first came to live with us, he seemed really nice, but over time I found him to be more dangerous than others she had brought home.

"Diana, you sit and rest, let me handle this." He offered.

"Tammy, ya ready?" His drawl was so Southern that I practically heard him singing the question to me. "Ya know we're gonna go 0 X 0 all the way through 12 X 12 and for every one ya miss, we're goin' to your bedroom, shutin' the door and you'll get a belt whippin'. That's right, for every one," he explained. Back into the room I followed, completely unaware that an offer of a belt or other consequences is what he had in mind. I was oblivious to what awaited me. He made sure that Momma heard the whippings, but not the other.

"Momma, please don't make me do this anymore!" I begged her after coming out, tears pouring down my face with a new level of fear and dread of those flash cards.

"Shut up, Tammy, and leave your momma alone. "Get o'er here and let's go through these cards again," he demanded.

"Momma, please?" I begged still crying, but she assumed it was because I didn't want any more whip-pings. I tried to tell her he was hurting me under my breath, but she couldn't hear me. She ordered me on.

"Come here, girl!" He teased me while forcing me to continue my learning with him. At times, tired of hearing him scold me, Momma even got mad at me for not responding quickly enough.

"Tammy, quit ignoring him! Now get over there and learn your math!" she yelled. But still Momma didn't get it. I knew her getting riled would only make it worse, so we went through the cards a second time and he would demand me to follow him, yanking me by the arm until we were closed off yet again. The next time he took me into the room, it wasn't twenty something whippings, it was less, but he made sure there was more of the other than the whippings and promised me next time I said anything to Momma about wanting her to do it instead of him, he would make sure I got double of both options. Absolutely and without exception or hesitation I knew my multiplications the next day and I was careful not to ever ask for homework help on anything again, at least not in that home.

While not all of the visitors Momma brought home affected me directly, there were plenty that did, and on occasion, some affected me indirectly. Nothing went unnoticed in my eyes. After I reached age nine, I started scrutinizing every person that began walking into my house. I don't have a vivid memory of every man that Momma brought home with the exception of a few. Usually the reason I remember anyone in particular is because of an undesirable act. Although there was one that stood out because he was different from the rest. Thank goodness his eyes were only on Momma and he didn't move in. I only saw him the one time, but I would never forget him either. They came in late from the bar and he spent the night. The next day when we awoke, he didn't walk out of her room like all the rest; lazy and sluggish, exposing more skin than necessary and bad personal hygiene. Instead, he was sitting at the table fully dressed in a nice shirt and shorts and sat quietly minding his own business while we ate. This guy was far nicer and cleaner than the rest. I was so excited at first because he was different. I couldn't recall a time that one willingly, through use of their own vehicle, offered to take us to Wal-Mart to buy groceries. Momma added to the excitement by promising a surprise for each of us and that was all the explanation she gave Sam Jr. and me.

I didn't figure it out at first. We had finished getting groceries and were about to check out when Momma told us that we could get a surprise like a cola and candy bar or bag of chips. We were so excited. Momma stopped in an aisle to pick out a magazine and while she was searching I began looking through the workbooks for kids. Picking up a $4 math workbook, I asked Momma if I could get it instead of the snack.

Surprising me by his tone, John, very aggravated, replied, "No way am I spending my money on that."

Momma looked at him very sternly and said, "You've already received your payment, she's getting the workbook."

Her voice was so demanding as if payment truly had been given...something stronger than money. My eyes watered up as I stood frozen with reality and disappointment.

"I don't want the stupid workbook," I said to John while placing it back on the rack and walking towards my mother.

In a hushed tone, I walked up to Momma, putting myself between her and John, "Momma, please leave these kind of people alone. We don't need their help. We'll be fine without them," I pleaded, knowing I was stepping over the line, but desperate to get her to listen.

"Tammy, don't be silly. John is just a friend and he wants to buy that book for you. Now quit it. Here..." she said as she reached back on the shelf and retrieved it before handing it to me. When I refused to take it, she threw it in the cart and as quickly as possible, limped her way towards the checkout line.

Again, I wasn't able to fully comprehend what was happening in my family. Momma had always assured us we would take care of each other; that we couldn't trust anyone and had told me on more than one occasion, "Tammy, everybody is always out for something." Thank God I would learn my own view on this opinion. The great thing was that Momma's perception was based on what she chose to find in life and I would, in time, find my own. I know now that there are many good people who give to others not wanting anything at all in return. I have been blessed in my lifetime to know many! If we set our eyes on the Lord and not man, we will find hope and peace.

Jeremiah 29:11 (NKJV)
For I know the thoughts that I think towards you, says the Lord, thoughts of peace and not of evil, to give you a future and a hope.

Chapter 4 – Middle School

It seemed our lives as a family would mirror that of a gypsy's family; Momma always running from trouble only to find more. During the summer following my third grade year we moved back to Iowa after Momma married the mayor of a small town. I'm not sure how she met him and the marriage only lasted a month before being annulled. Following the brief relationship we moved to a rental home in the same town with an elevator and a ghost that fancied turning on water faucets randomly upstairs. We stayed in Iowa for the remaining year allowing me to complete the fourth grade there. Because we only attended one year, I found it difficult to make friends. The year was a blur with everything unfamiliar and no real sense of home, except for the school. It was named 'Mentzer Elementary,' which suited me just fine.

Before the fifth grade started Momma pulled us back to Alabama. This time to the town of Leeds, which was located at the bottom of the mountain just a few miles from Dunnavant. I would attend Leeds Elementary School for my fifth and sixth grade years. I continued to find it difficult to make friends in the school and my distaste for academia continued to grow. This was evidenced by a steady decline in performance in the classroom, consisting of my first really awful report card including Ds and Fs. During this time my greatest discoveries came outside the classroom.

I discovered that I loved sports, softball in particular. I not only loved it, I excelled at it. Possibly it was an opportunity to release aggressions or a place I found acceptance. I'm not sure of the reasons, but I was motivated. In the beginning it was a curiosity; eventually it was a drive within. Many times, especially at first, I had to walk to all the events — practices and games — but I didn't miss. Through my dedication and abilities, I earned the league MVP while I played. I loved having the opportunity to feel normal, like any other person. It was a city league and not associated with the school, so all the fights, suspensions, and general trouble I got into at school had no repercussions there. It wasn't me against the world when I was on the field; I was part of the world. Because I walked to get to practice, it was easy for me to pretend that only my coach knew where I came from. The girls accepted me on the field because I could help carry the team, so if they looked down on me, they didn't show it there.

Momma took advantage of my willingness to walk to practice. She sent me on frequent errands of walking to the store and once a month she would walk with me to the bank which was a round trip of slightly over 4 miles. This had to be a difficult walk on Momma's gimpy leg, but she never complained, probably because she was focused on her once-a-month income that would restock our groceries and curb her nicotine crave. What I remember most, besides the long walk hiking back with bags of groceries in hand, is the teller, Mrs. Joyce. A beautiful, middle aged woman who always greeted my mother with respect.

"Hello, Ms. Mentzer. How are you today?"

"Fine, Joyce," she would reply with a nice smile, always followed with, "and you?"

"I am good. Did you walk again?" she would ask each time. Usually Momma answered with a yes, but on occasion she would proudly brag of a friend or relative that aided the ride that day.

"How much this month, Joyce?" Momma would ask, knowing that her account was more than likely overdrawn again.

"Let me look," she would reply and begin typing at a machine to retrieve the data for her.

"I am so sorry. I don't know how this keeps happening." Momma would usually apologize with a very sincere and somewhat embarrassed excuse.

"You don't worry about it, Ms. Mentzer. We know your check will come in. I just wish you would save a little so that you wouldn't get charged these fees. Here, let me see what I can do to put some of that back in for you."

"Thank you, Joyce. You're a real nice person. Thank you. I've got to buy some food, ya know. And pay bills. This will help."

"No problem, Ms. Mentzer, just try to be careful with those fees. We can't always give them back."

"I know," Momma would respond.

I was never embarrassed by Momma overdrawing the account. Maybe I didn't understand how disgraceful that could've been perceived, but I was very aware of how nice Mrs. Joyce was to my mother. She treated her with respect. A very well-dressed and well-kept woman who did not act like she was any better than my mother, but instead handled Momma's banking business as a valued customer. Later in life, my first real job interview would be at a bank in Birmingham, Alabama for a teller position. I remember the Human Resources lady asking me why I should be considered over the other interested people for their position of teller. I shared with her the story of my familiarity with banking and of Joyce and how I knew I could be that kind of teller.

Friends were hard to come by at school as I always felt like the outsider. But at home in the apartment complex I discovered a friend that accepted me for who I was — whose friendship wouldn't hinge on whom else was around or what other people said. It was a friendship that wouldn't fade from memory with the next move. It was a lifelong friendship. I discovered Jen. We had so much in common, from seeing the very first music video of Billy Idol, to dressing up Barbies. Unlike the girls at our school, our Barbies did not have the store-bought, pink plastic outdoor pool made for dolls, but instead, a large salad bowl that converted to our needs just fine. The water stayed and the Barbies were able to dip.

Jen also came from a single-parent home. To me, her mother was like the quintessential German lady. Renate was tall and stocky, but not too big. And she was not going to be pushed around. Strong in mind and strong in will. She spoke with a thick German accent, which at times could require a great deal of focus to understand, as the words at first seemed to blend together very indiscriminately. It was a beautiful accent and although I was focused intently on what she said, I almost always realized I was smiling while I listened. Renate just had that affect as she possessed one of the most genuine spirits of kindness that always came forth when she spoke, and then of course, there was her contagious smile. Renate had another side too. If her temper flared up, we stayed in Jen's room out of the way. Normally that would only happen when Jennifer had been watching her little brother and aggravating him so badly that when their mother would return home Renate would discover that they had been fighting.

While my brother, Sam, and Jen's brother, David, were several years apart, Jennifer and I only held one year difference between the two of us and we bonded immediately. The most engaging thing about her friendship, besides her availability to hang out, was her laugh. Jennifer enjoyed life and she had such a creative streak to her that everything around her was an escape for me into make believe instead of reality.

The apartment complex we resided in was government subsidized and rather large for the little town of Leeds. It included an outdoor pool where Jen taught me to swim. The apartments were surrounded by a small wooded area that we would ride our bikes through or build forts in and we would even go dumpster diving. While not often, we did occasionally jump into the dumpsters to see what goodies had been tossed. We were usually looking for treasures such as clothes thrown out but not worn out, toys in working order, or anything that with a little imagination and ingenuity could be turned into something useful. Occasionally we would hit pay dirt.

"Oh my gosh, Jen, look at this!" I squealed with pleasure, lifting a large pile of typed white pages up out of the mix of trash.

"What is that?" she questioned, taking it from me and examining it. "Can you believe someone threw this away? All that hard work and they threw it away?" Jennifer sat there admiring the volumes of manuscript pages, neatly typed and numbered.

"You want to take it and read it?" I urged her to agree.

"Yeah. Gee, I just can't believe they threw this away." she said, forgetting that anything else might be found. With curiosity we emerged from the dumpster and headed up to her apartment. Quickly discovering some curse words, Jen decided to hide the pages until later that night, after her mom went to sleep. The day went by quickly and when night time came, we held an initiation of sorts before the official reading.

"Okay, it's time to initiate." I called. We looked at each with that all too familiar mischievous look then headed off into her kitchen.

"Just one rule…we really have to do it this time. I mean, we have to drink it. Let's see…" Jen pondered while searching through the cabinets.

With the refrigerator opened, I asked for agreement on the orange juice.

"Definitely." She replied. "Hey, what about this?" She asked as she pulled out different spices including hot sauce and black pepper, each new spice bringing with it its introduction and arch of the eyebrow or a wrinkle of the nose.

"Oh yeah, and what about this?" I asked, retrieving the mustard and an egg.

In agreement we continued to pull out ketchup, Worcestershire sauce and anything else we could find in the cabinet that could be ingested. Just a little bit of each, mixed up in a glass to make a nasty concoction that would challenge us to successfully drink. Yes, we both choked our small drink all the way down. Initiation for the night was over.

After her mom went to sleep, we did try to read the book, although I don't think we got very far. Being a little more grown up for us than our minds were ready for, we bored with it, only finding brief interest in dirty words that we normally did not have the liberty to read and an occasional challenge word due to our age and inexperience in more complicated vocabulary.

Jen and I got in a lot of sleepovers during those two years. This was influenced by our moms' affinity of running to the bars on the weekends. While my mother had never given much thought to it, Renate thought it to be a good idea for Jen and me to be together on those nights. We didn't object. While Momma and Renate would keep late hours, the company kept had changed. Things were definitely different in the context of whom Momma befriended and brought home.

Just before the completion of my sixth grade, Momma got a call that no one expected. From Iowa, the child that was taken while Momma was in a coma had found us. We were given something we had been missing. A long lost son and brother. It was his eighteenth birthday and he was rummaging through his father's things when he discovered that his mother was not his mother, but that Diana Mentzer was. He set out to find her and did so successfully. Momma was over visiting with Renate when Jim called.

Ring, ring, ring. Running around the corner, Sam answered the phone.

"Hello?"

"What? Really?" Sam continued before yelling for me, "Sis, get in here, now. Go get Momma—hurry!"

"What?" I asked, confused, walking into the kitchen with no sense of urgency.

"It's Jimmy. Go get Mom!"

"Who?"

"Here," he said, rather frustrated, "hold this and don't hang up. It's Jim. I'm going to get Mom."

"Hello."

"Who is this, Diana?" questioned the voice on the other end of the phone.

"No, this is Tammy."

"Who?"

"Tammy, her daughter. Who are you?"

"Are you crapping me?" he asked. "Crap!" he went on. "Holy cow, I have a brother and a sister? Dang!" he added.

"Hey, this isn't funny. Who is this?" I insisted, perplexed about who knew about Momma's little boy. Momma had said that when we were old enough she would go and find him. According to her, her ex-husband, who caused her head injury, took her child away from her while she was in the coma and ran away with his mistress. She talked about it on and off but we never knew whether or not to believe her. He was never around anyway, so why would we?

"I'll be. I have a sister and a brother," he said with a sincere laugh of surprise.

"Is this some joke? Tell me who you are." I demanded.

"No joke, Sis. This is your brother Jimmy."

"Listen, this is not funny. My momma doesn't need this prank. You don't know my momma. She can't handle a prank like this. Now tell me who this is."

"Seriously, girl, I am not kidding. Tammy? Right? I am your brother, Jimmy R W. and I just found out about Mom."

49

A Teacher's Prayer

Instantly I felt calm. There was something Momma hadn't entirely made up. Something that was true. Since Dad's death, I had heard numerous versions about my father drinking and the likes. Then I heard other things I perceived as made up, such as about how my grandparents were always trying to have us taken away from our momma. That stacked on how everybody in the world was out to get us. Even though she told the questionable story of her long-lost son often enough, it was nice to know beyond a shadow of a doubt it was true. Especially since it was hard to imagine a mother not knowing where her own child was. A sense of joy and relief began to take root, while I waited there for Momma to return home. Momma would no longer have to wait until we grew up to find her other child. There was nothing more I could say to him; after all, I didn't know him well enough to talk much, so I asked him to hold, and assured him it wouldn't be long before Momma returned home. As soon as she entered the apartment, she took the phone from my hand. Putting the receiver up to her ear, tears poured down her face as she realized she was reuniting with her baby boy of eighteen lost years.

That week, Momma took some money out of the trust and we flew up to visit our brother. Shortly after we got in his car he demonstrated for us one of the differences between driving in the North and driving in the South. Whirling around a grocery store parking lot, covered in ice, he introduced us to a different type of donut than Krispy Kreme. He scared Momma badly as she braced her hands to the ceiling, arms fully extended and all the while screaming. Sam and I found the thrill in it, laughing while leaned into each other's laps and against the doors at each turn. We thoroughly enjoyed the few seconds it lasted. Jimmy continued his display of the art of handling a car, assuring Momma we were all going to be okay. Although, if memory serves me well, between his wife and my mother, he only spun around a few times more because Momma wouldn't quit yelling at him. Maybe it was because the only times we were in an automobile were on the bus for church or school or in my grandparents car (outside Momma's few men friends the few times they drove us for groceries); and nobody drove us like what you saw on the movies. Not until Jim.

While at the time I didn't realize it, it appeared the apple didn't fall far from the tree. Jim was so happy to meet us and respectively we were just as pleased to finally meet him. It wouldn't take long to determine that Jim lived quite a wild night life, but he was all heart! At six feet tall and two hundred-twenty pounds of muscular build, a few tattoos and what I considered to be a good looking guy, he was like a kid trapped in a man's body. I would later learn that mentality to be a cause from drug abuse that had been present in his life for several years. While we enjoyed our visit, it was short-lived and we had to return home to Alabama, but in no time we would pack up again and move to be near Jim.

During these two years of my fifth and sixth grades, it appears life was really about finding true friends, family, and confidence. I was never abused, touched, or violated. Looking back, I believe that Renate's time and influence with my mother created a shroud of protection around me that I had not seen since my father died. But it was not to last, as Momma, getting restless, decided it was time to move again. The shroud was gone but Renate and Jennifer's impact on my life would last forever. I know, however, the reason Momma moved us to Iowa that summer was to be with Jim. It was supposed to be our final move. The two week visit with Jim was exciting, but to move and leave Jennifer, my best friend, seemed as real of a loss as losing my father. Lucky for me, she and I would keep in touch from that day forward. Our friendship was a special one, kept by letters and phone calls, and when moves would accommodate, visits too.

My seventh grade year was spent back in Iowa with our family trying to become whole again. We lived in Cedar Rapids where I had to ride a city bus to school, which was quite intimidating. It wasn't the snobby kids picking on me there, it was grownups that made me uncomfortable. The adults were a lot older than I was, and they were not about laughing and cutting up. Say what you like, but I would have felt safer with the snobby kids picking on me, than the closed-off man reading his paper who didn't even acknowledge the lady sitting next to him. It was quite a different ride and a very uncomfortable one, especially when we would get to the station and have to wait on the bus to unload and reload, crowding the aisles with even more adults. Very few children rode our bus. I guess everyone else's parents could drive. The school itself sat at the top of a hill facing the main road and overlooked the city. It was McKinley Jr. High School and it reminded me of the school on the movie, *Lean on Me.* Coming from a K-12 school, it was quite overwhelming to be inside a school facility that housed its own auditorium and music room and gym (each individual rooms). The halls were lined with lockers that were beaten up and decorated sporadically with graffiti. It was a multiple-level building, very large, with so many different types of classes that it was quite the eye opener for a country girl. At this school, in seventh grade, I was able to take algebra and typing. Even though I had completed these courses in Iowa, I would not be allowed to take them again until ninth grade in Alabama. That year I learned a lot about survival. Old enough to have to protect myself in school from fights and different enough with my Southern accent that I drew attention from people I didn't want it from. I was glad to not go back there, so when Momma's and Jim's relationship did not pan out in story-book fashion, this time I was ready to move.

After we did not get the happy ending with Jim as we had hoped, it became obvious that Momma had a lot of built-up resentment against certain behaviors—probably that his dad had left forever scarred upon her heart. Unfortunately, it would get in the way of her ability to love Jim as he wanted her to; but if he only knew, Momma's love was limited all the way around, yet it was sincere.

Jim loved to party and that included quite a bit of substance abuse and alcohol. Momma just couldn't tolerate the constant presence of weed and drugs, but the alcohol was not only welcomed in our home but offered on special occasions, even to me. During our stay I would learn that most of the habits Jim had, he said he learned from his dad. His and Momma's fights escalated in frequency and duration until it all eventually came to a boiling point. This was the point at which Momma couldn't take it any more and didn't want to try. She packed us up and moved us back to our first home in Alabama—back into the house we built with Daddy's money, and right back next to my grandparents.   This was my last move with Momma, but not my last move.

Romans 8: 28 (LASB)
And we know that God causes everything
to work together for the good of those who love God
and are called according to his purpose for them.

Chapter 5 – Last Stay in Dunnavant

Living again in Dunnavant, I would attend my eighth through the first semester of tenth grade at Chelsea High School. In that time, I would come to appreciate just how mean kids could be to one another. In the teenage years, youth are focused on their peers, trying to find the perfect fit of friends to hang out with. Sometimes that means pointing out just how different other kids are. My school bus ride to and from school would consist of teenagers making fun of me by name-calling and teasing; pointing out my differences and imperfections as they saw it. I had a huge crush on an older classmate that rode the same bus. Once the girls on the bus found out, they started teasing me—and him—all the time. It would embarrass me terribly, but he would just laugh it off. The teases ranged from, "Go ahead and kiss her," to "You know if you kissed her, her breathe alone would kill you." Unfortunately my breath *was* a problem but I didn't know it. At age fifteen, I had not been to the dentist more than one time in my entire life and that was to have a rotten tooth pulled by a student at the UAB clinic. I just thought those kids were being mean and they just thought that I was nasty. What were they being taught at home to care so little about someone else, and what was I being taught at home to be so unaware of caring for myself? I earned a new nickname on that bus too. It was used to address me on more than one occasion; "Here comes Greaseball!" they would say while knocking at the back of my head as I sat in my seat. Or upon entering the bus, they would belittle me because of my oily hair.

A Teacher's Prayer

"Hey, Greaseball. Come sit here," they would offer, patting the seat in front or to the side of them.

"No nasty girl ain't sitting by me. You do not sit here, Greaseball!" always it seemed a girl would chime in. Maybe that is why I preferred to play backyard football with the guys and tomboys of our neighborhood.

"Dang, you smell," someone else would call out as I passed by.

While their words seem horrible and cruel to recollect, it can't be avoided that they were, to some effect, true. They were expressing all they knew of me because they didn't really know me. I was too different to get to know. I am confident that those kids did not know that I didn't wash my hair more than once a week because we couldn't afford shampoo and that our mother liked to have her hair smelling good when she went out to the bars to cater to her alcoholic tendencies. I learned a lot from the kids on the bus. Not the obvious 'I need to take better care of my hygiene.' I learned that my words have a profound impact on someone else's life by the way their words affected me. If they had only chosen a kind word instead, how different my memory would be.

With no real guidance and very few friends during this time, the interactions seemed to become more intense. New and different methods of survival would begin to take flight in me and would manifest in anger. All of my energy from home and from my peers would normally come to a head, causing many fights on the bus as well as at school. I spent more than my fair share of time in the Principal's office…a common theme at Chelsea for me: the Principal and a paddle.

A Teacher's Prayer

Another contributor to my attitude would be protecting my brother—around whom most of my fights revolved. The mean brother, who would wail me with a sucker punch in the stomach at home, when I wasn't looking, or hit me on the side of the head with whatever he could find, like a large jar of peanut butter, would tend to get picked on a whole lot at school. I was just sick of it all. Sam was held back several years until finally quitting school at age sixteen in the eighth grade. I never really physically held my own against him until I figured out I could beat up the kids at school that picked on him. After this was established the bullying at home ceased. I would keep going to school at Chelsea, riding the bus through my first semester of tenth grade.

As I got older I learned to look for my regulars— my friends that would save me a seat. When they weren't on the bus, my misfortune became more miserable. Friends have a way of keeping us preoccupied with laughter and stories from the day before. Whether it was fighting with their brothers and sisters, telling about being irritated at their mom and dad, gossiping about the latest hometown news or sharing their secrets of their newest crush, they could help to drown out all of the noise of the uppities. Uppities was the name my friends gave to the young people that wore clothes without stains or tears, very clean shoes and those that usually had more than one pair to alternate. They always had snack money and hung out with the so-called popular crowd. They were of upper class, sometimes middle, and wouldn't usually associate with our socio-economic group, unless it was to tease. As I got older, more times than not, I ignored them and they left me alone.

A Teacher's Prayer

It was my tenth grade year when I began focusing on how and when to quit school. It was somewhere between ages eleven and fourteen that I believed school to be a waste of time. I didn't understand the purpose of it. I watched kids get to play in sports and band while I simply wished I had those opportunities. Since Momma couldn't drive, and the boyfriends she bought cars for didn't stick around, I had to catch a bus home each day after school because there were no rides going my way if I were to stay for an activity. If I missed the bus, I knew there would be serious consequences, such as whippings and scolding, because we didn't have a car and there was no way I could walk the winding, thirty mile stretch to my house. The closer fifteen years of age approached, the more I realized what I had to do—forget school. It may be important for some people, but it definitely would not suffice for me. My goal was to turn sixteen and quit school like Sam did. He didn't have to put up with the crap with the other kids anymore and I wouldn't have to either. I wouldn't have to get up early to catch a bus and I would be able to go to work at McDonald's. I remember very clearly getting so excited thinking about bringing home around a hundred bucks a week and being able to get a used car. I could take Momma to the zoo and drive to the lake to go swimming. I could also get a Big Mac and shake whenever I wanted. At fifteen, I could count on both hands with fingers left over how many times I had been given that opportunity. I couldn't turn sixteen fast enough! At that time, I thought that was successful: a job, a used car and an opportunity to go to the zoo or drive over to the lake. I had no clue how much more life held for me because no one had taken the time to show me. Not every memory from Chelsea

High School was bad. Not everyone was mean. The negative voices were almost always the loudest and so easily drowned out the ones who could make a difference and provide a glimpse of hope and love.

I received free lunches due to Momma's income and was given a new lunch ticket every so often to get food with. My only responsibility was to keep up with the tickets and ensure I had them at lunchtime or else there would be no meal for the day. After all, I was old enough. There were times when I lost it or forgot it and at first the school let me borrow money, but soon they learned I couldn't pay them back (and wouldn't). So they stopped loaning the money and explained that I needed to learn to remember to keep up with my lunch ticket—that I needed to become more responsible for myself. The school lunch was a very important meal because at this point Momma no longer had much money left at her disposal, and what she did have was mostly drank away or drained by her boyfriends. There were so many days that we'd go without a good supper, or even breakfast, because we were low on food and had to make it last until the third of the next month when we had our monthly grocery trip. Usually I could handle it; my appetite had gotten used to not having large portions, but there were times I couldn't fill myself enough. At 5'7" and less than 100 pounds, it didn't take much to fill my stomach. The lack of food may have also been a contributor to my anger level at the time. Some days I would go to school so hungry, unable to concentrate, and ill—my stomach literally hurting, counting the minutes until the lunch hour would come, my mouth watering and yearning for something with flavor. We may have had some food at home but there were many times that I was desperate for a salad at school or even a greasy, rectangular, pepperoni pizza, which I always looked forward to.

There were days when I was sitting at school, eating my salad, tears silently trailing down my face because I felt so guilty for eating while Momma sat at home with nothing more than butterbeans and eggs to cook. We usually had eggs and frequently had chicken because we raised chickens along with my grandparents. While I liked eggs and assisted in gathering them, I had witnessed my grandfather killing a chicken and found that I could no longer eat the meat. More times than not, we would run out of food at home before the next paycheck would come. On occasion I stuffed wrapped crackers into my pocket and carrot sticks sealed in a napkin to take home to Momma. It was amazing that I thought bringing her this napkin-wrapped food would make her happy and prove to her that we could take care of each other without help from the outside. I thought of the carrot sticks as fancy food and looked forward to seeing her expression when I got home to present the gift. How many kids today sit there at school, eating their free lunches, but not enjoying it due to the guilt of their parents not having the same pleasure? It truly is something to think about in a country where many of us have the luxury to take food for granted, even throw away what we choose not to eat. If we paid more attention we would see there are a lot of hungry people, including children, in our country today.

On the days that I forgot my ticket, usually I would sit and watch while everybody else ate. Most times it didn't matter because I wasn't hungry. Yet one day I was so hungry that I just sat at the cafeteria table, being mad at myself for being irresponsible and not paying more attention to what I walked out of the house with that morning. I was fifteen and had no excuse for being so absent-minded, I thought. As I sat on the round stool, slouched over the table, face staring down but resting in my hands, someone walked up behind me.

"Tammy, are you okay?" a young female voice asked. After a short time of no response, she placed her hand on my shoulder and said, "Aren't you going to eat?" I quickly gathered myself and in a very sarcastic voice responded, "Well, not today, I can't find my ticket."

She then asked, "Well, don't you have any money?"

I wanted to turn around and say, *are you kidding?* But instead, I simply responded under my breath, "No." I actually started getting angry. Couldn't she see I didn't have any food? Didn't she know how hungry I was? What was it to her? Her questions were making my stomach hurt worse and all I wanted her to do was go away. I could feel the anger rising, not at her, but at me. All the same it was rising.

"Well, I have some you can borrow." I turned in disbelief wondering who in the world was talking to me, a little ashamed of my pent-up anger. I didn't recognize the voice as any of my teachers and as I turned, I saw Tiffany reach into her purse and pull out one dollar and ten cents. She handed it to me with a great big smile and then walked on. She never even waited for a thank you and not once did she ever ask me to pay the money back.

I was very surprised. I didn't know Tiffany very well, but I did know she was a very pretty, petite classmate who was a good cheerleader, or so I thought at the time. I would later discover that she only cheered in our younger days, but in high school her love was softball. Tiffany hung out with the popular crowd, so our paths never really crossed until that day. I went to school with her awhile longer following that event and on more than one occasion she came to my rescue—a few times with lunch money, and on occasion telling her friends to leave me alone. We didn't become friends, but she did demonstrate that trait just by her action. Tiffany was not just an acquaintance, but someone who reached out to me in loving kindness. I still think of her often and the impact she had on me. She wasn't afraid to stand up for the less fortunate. Where did she learn to be kind? One of the most impressionable memories of my childhood was this girl's kindness, even amongst her friends. She was herself—she was com-passionate and still popular. Funny thing is that I don't think that made her any less in her own friends' eyes. They seemed to also respect her in a way that I am not sure anyone at our age could understand. I would leave home in my tenth grade year and she would become the example for the type of person I wanted to become. The lesson I learned from her is to be myself regardless of who is around. In doing so, I might actually be aware of opportunities to help others that have a need. Chances are if you are true to yourself and not doing things so that people will notice then you are able to be yourself and not be judged for doing so. We are only judged by others when in our minds we allow them to pass judgment on us. I happen to believe that the key might have been that she was so comfortable with who she was that she didn't care what people thought. I found out a few years later, that by not caring what people thought, life is so much more fun and rewarding!

Matthew 25:34-35, 40 (NRSV)

The king will say to those at his right hand,
"…I was a stranger and you welcomed me…just as you did it to one of the least of these who are members of my family, you did it to me."

Chapter 6 - My Final Stay

Moving back to Dunnavant brought with it Momma's return to old habits, including both an increase in bar visits and in different men coming and going. I was old enough, in my mind, to come and go as I pleased, so as long as I had a friend's house I could crash at, I would. There were still times I had to deal with life at home, but not nearly as much. The security of that home, though, was not an option either.

The older I became the more self conscience I became. I started wearing oversize shirts trying to hide any evidence that might attract the older, opposite sex. I hated my reflection in the mirror, although I didn't realize how lonely and sad my eyes were, how unkempt my hair was or how ridiculously my makeup had been applied. I remember just wishing not to be pretty at all, and then no-one would notice me. At that time of my life, I had a little more control, but still not completely. I was older and understood even better the dangers around me. I was sick of the nasty yellow-stained teeth that didn't know when to quit smiling at me. Life was so unbearable at my mother's house. Momma's friends weren't at all like mine and made it a necessity to grow up quickly. Either it was the men cornering me in a room alone to explain what they expected of me or it was them offering gifts of safety for my family if I would cooperate with them and not tell anyone. I feared these particular bribes because so many of these men had already visited jail or prison. I would later discover how lucky I was because one of Momma's boyfriends that was living with us did go to prison for murdering a teenage girl.

64

A Teacher's Prayer

This life took an innocent, spirited child and turned her into a closed-off young woman. Early in life, self-preservation became an internal drive and a defining force for me—one which formed a definition of which I would be the only one to comprehend its true implications on my life. Yet the grace of God didn't just happen; it sustained me and brought me through it. Had it not been for the hope in someone—something better and greater than all imagined, someone forgiving—I am confident I wouldn't have made it through those years.

I believe it was during my ninth grade year that Sam Jr. became a deliberate rebel out to defy our mother in any way possible. Within a short time of his announced rebellion, my brother was placed into a detention home and a social worker was assigned to us. Then another, then another. It wasn't until the fourth or fifth social worker that one finally asked, "How are you doing Tammy? You can talk to me about anything and I want you to know that." She repeated this approach time and again, assuring me of total confidentiality if I chose to open up. In hindsight, others might have, I really don't recall, but I do remember this. At first, I thought she was just doing her job. In a way, making cordial 'to dos' over everyone in the family. Yet her persistence forced me to start trying to figure her out. While doing so, I guess it was time for me to open up, because this is when I first started to realize that things going on at my house were not okay.

On Dunnavant Mountain we took care of our family. What happened at home, stayed at home. As long as my momma knew and could do nothing about it then no one else could either. I just didn't realize that in fact, it wasn't normal for a girl of my age to have been through the things that I had. Sure, deep down in my gut, I figured as much. The concept of right versus wrong was not lost on me, but why would all of this be allowed otherwise? Your home is a place where family takes care of family and no one else has your best interest in mind. Sam came and went, running away a couple of times as well as being removed by the State. This tension between Momma and Sam would cause me to seek solace elsewhere.

During the summer leading up to my tenth grade year I began attending a new church. It was a Revival Center in Leeds where we had church every night of the week. I clung to this escape, but it was here my relationship with the Lord developed to a new level. I started reading scripture on my own and learned new styles of worship. Going to church there every night would instill a second family in my life and I would hope to find shelter and solace within those white walls.

At first it didn't shield me from all of the emptiness and desperation of my home when I would return. In fact, on more than one occasion I had handwritten a will on a piece of notebook paper for my friends, and would tuck it under my pillow or set it on the nightstand to be found in the morning when Momma came to awake me unsuccessfully. A will which included every detail from cassette tapes to shoes, etc. A will thankfully that would never be needed. I remember trying to swallow enough pills to get my troubles over, but praying myself asleep before I could finish. No telling how many different times or quantities I ingested. Never enough to work and never enough to send me to the hospital. And I remember more horrid details of self destruction to end the pain I was experiencing. Yet each time my prayers, a phone call from a friend, or my school counselor's prodding would provide enough relief to see me through another day.

My guidance counselor called me to the office at Chelsea High School. I had a visitor and as I walked into a room and the door shut behind me, I met a very kind man. This was my tenth grade year and oddly enough he just happened to show up one day after I prayed through taking pills and falling asleep. I was only told that he would like to speak with me for a minute and nothing else. At school the adults never hurt me, so I had no guard up with him in a room, besides he was nicely dressed and kept his space while we talked. I can't explain to this day why he chose that day to come and speak to me, but as it turned out, he was a counselor.

"Tammy," he started introducing himself, "some of your teachers are worried about you."

"They are?" I questioned, curious to where he was going.

"Yeah, they are. Should they be?" he asked me softly and not challenging in any way. If I had not just had a really bad night, I probably wouldn't have admitted anything to him. I had interviewed with many social workers and not divulged things, but I was getting tired and desperate for someone to help.

"Well, I don't know," I responded, not sure what to say.

"Well, what I am asking is, are you okay?" he continued.

"I guess."

"I'm not so sure you are. I am here because I think you need a friend and I want you to know that you can say anything to me and I will keep it between us. Okay?"

"Okay," I replied, still not sure that I wanted to admit to anything.

"So, Tammy, can I ask you a personal question?" he continued. The next question he asked stunned me. I am not sure how he knew to ask; maybe he could read it on my face, in my eyes, maybe I had said something to a friend who reported me to a teacher, or something, but for the life of me I couldn't disregard his question with a dishonest answer because I needed someone to know.

"Have you ever tried to take your life?"

With that question, tears began, but only barely.

"Yes," I responded, "I tried last night."

"How, Tammy?"

We sat there in silence then he continued, "Was it with pills?"

"How do you know?" I asked, connecting with him because of the shock that he could possibly know without me telling him, without me telling anyone.

I don't remember the rest of our conversation outside of us talking for quite awhile and for whatever reason, his being able to build up a trust in me. That day, he gave me a business card and told me to keep it in my purse so that if I ever needed him, to call and he would talk to me; he would be my friend. I thanked him and left the office. No one besides the guidance counselor saw us talking so there was no embarrassment to the conversation which probably helped me to hold on to the card and not tear it up, as I had done with others. Not long after that meeting, I would experience one of the most brutal ideas for harming myself, but because he gave me a card, would be able to work my way through it. Within two weeks from that event I would start my life over and thank God, never revisit those kinds of self-destructing thoughts.

As stated, during the summer leading up to my sophomore year, I had learned to pray. I had started going back to church and one day I developed a new prayer while sitting at the television, watching an idealistic not-so-normal family show, The Facts of Life. I remember going to bed one night and telling the Lord how cool it would be if I could live in a group home like that. I could be Jo. She was tough like I was, yet she was happy, as I wanted to be. I knew it was ridiculous but I had been taught to speak with God about anything.

Being a small church, with membership of about thirty or so and at least one third being youth, it wasn't hard to get to know people within the building. Adults and children would come together to worship as well as to study the Bible. What may have been one of the most attractive aspects to me was the fact that I was equally welcomed to study the Bible with adults and not separate from them. I developed some dear friendships, in particular with my pastor, Sister Maria (this is not her real name). Other friendships were more of an acquaintance, but all the same, Godly and trustworthy, or at least they were supposed to be. During that summer, a younger couple—a man and woman probably somewhere in their late-twenties to mid-thirties—started befriending me. We spent lots of time together at church studying the Bible, particularly Revelation.

At this time, I still lived on Dunnavant Mountain and had it not been for Sister Maria picking me up and taking me home, I wouldn't have gotten to go to church. While only about twelve miles from Leeds, the road was heavily elevated with many hairpin curves to traverse. The roads were too dangerous to ride bikes down with oncoming traffic. The young couple started offering to pick me up and take me home, to help Sister Maria. After several times of doing this, they offered to let me come spend a week with them during the summer, since I was out of school and they had learned my family was unable to take vacations. My mother, without so much as meeting them, gave permission for me to do so and the next night I packed my bags along with my excitement and was picked up yet again for church.

It was near the end of summer and I was glad to finally being doing something. I also didn't see it as odd because like I said, our church was a small family-like group. The first night at their home was fun. Being away from my own home was always comforting, but getting undivided attention from two adults who seemed so sweet was also assuring. I remember we would walk downtown to the grocery store to get a soda or we would go out and work on his car, while he would explain to me the difference of bearings and engine things — none of which I remember details about today. I also remember they lived with his mother, which really wasn't so odd considering my own background, where my circle tended to stick around because we just couldn't make it on our own. He had several brothers, one of which was in prison for murder and another who was a couple of years older than I was and who I found attractive. Needless to say, I thought I was going to have a great time with them that week.

A Teacher's Prayer

When we left church the second night, they began reading scriptures to me and teaching me by Biblical stories, lessons they believed to be divine inspiration from God and had the pleasure to teach many other young ladies. Up to this point in my life, I thought if someone could back up what they said with scripture, the God-breathed Word, then it must have been sent straight from Him. I would later learn that not to be true. That night and the next day they read stories to me from the Old Testament of men who had multiple wives and numerous children. They told me of the corrupt world we lived in and how corrupt it had become and that God had called them to rebuild His people and His place on this earth by getting back to the basics of Old Testament teachings. I can't quote the scriptures they read to me but I can tell you they made me read from my own Bible along with them as they read out loud. I sat there stunned in disbelief because it didn't make sense, but these were good people that I went to church with who had never hurt me and they were reading scripture so it had to be the truth. They went on to say what they were going to do to me that night and why. Then they explained how we would all be moving to Texas to rejoin with his other community of believers and his other wives. At age fifteen I had never heard of cults or envisioned such a fallible and malicious use against God, but would soon discover how real that was.

That night after my natural female innocence was taken away from me in the name of God, I sat locked off in a bathroom with instructions of how to clean myself up and cried for what I know was at least an hour. I had no way to get home and was angry at God. I was disappointed, not understanding how He could allow something so against my own will. I could not understand why in the world He would tell them these things, but not tell me. I did not understand that Satan knows scripture. I obviously hadn't yet learned the story of Jesus in the wilderness and Satan using scripture to try and tempt Him, only to have Christ correctly state what the scripture meant. Just how many times is scripture taken out of context and for what human gain?

This is the reason I have little problem accepting that people do not come to church because of the people there. I could have easily turned my back on organized church, but the church is the collective group and it was after all the church who originally showed me the light to Christ in Vacation Bible School and would teach me so much goodness that I would have hope during hopeless times. As I grew, I would come to seek scripture for more answers and at some point come to realize that we can not put our eyes on man, for man will fail, but we are to set our eyes on God alone. We as humans assign value and judgment to so many things and it is just not our place. The valuable lesson I learned is that the Holy Spirit does reside with us once we accept Christ and are baptized new in Him; and if the Spirit within me is not feeling it, then it probably isn't of God. It's at least worth praying more about and searching more of. Not to leave you burdened, I will say that my self-preservation kicked in again and by the grace of God I would not see those people for much longer. The next day I was violently sick to my stomach so it wasn't hard to convince them I needed to call Momma for some medicine.

They gave me permission to do so and while I didn't really have the extreme migraine I pretended to, I was sick of being in that house. So I walked back downtown to the store where I used a pay phone to call Momma, insisting that she and grandfather come pick me up immediately. I begged her not to ask any questions at all and that once they arrived, to insist I go home for such severe headaches (of which I did have a history). I remember making Momma promise she would not leave without me and would ask absolutely no questions. Momma heard me crying and tried to get me to tell her what was going on, but I hung up and insisted she just come immediately. I knew she couldn't know, because one, I thought she wouldn't be able to handle it, and two, one of them was already in prison for murder. I knew I couldn't physically protect my own family, therefore saying nothing at all would be the best all the way around. Momma did show up without too much delay and I went home, never to see those people again, not even at church. I would love to tell you that we pressed charges, but before you jump to assumptions, please realize the fear a fifteen year old was bearing by herself to protect her family.

Tenth grade soon started and I continued to have troubles mount one upon another: from severe stomach issues to continued bad grades and harassment from other kids. I did let the pastor know and she cried with me and prayed with me, but not once did she encourage me to file a report with the police. Sister Maria assured me that their acts were not of God, but were evil. She believed that God would deal with them in His time. I never saw that couple again at that church and while I did begin pulling back from church at that point, I still attended there. I felt God had forsaken me and unfortunately thought I must have deserved it. Again, another misconception.

A Teacher's Prayer

(Ps 71:4-5 (NKJV)
Deliver me, O my God, out of the hand of the wicked, out of the
hand of the unrighteous and cruel man. For thou art my hope, O
Lord God: thou art my trust from my youth.

Chapter 7-Run Away

It was October of 1987, and I had no idea of how my life was about to change in a matter of a few weeks. The last year seemed to have spiraled out of control to land me in my current emotional abyss. I felt like I had hit rock bottom. My family was on the verge of crumbling away as my brother was determined to leave. My first semester of tenth grade would lay the groundwork for my decision to run away. It would be then that I would know — would discover — that God had not forsaken me after all. Neither the continued abuse and lack of trust which seemed to be waiting in every direction I turned, nor the hardened maturity and clearer understanding of right and wrong would be the catalyst when I finally decided to leave home. I was caught in an abuse cycle, and for whatever reason, felt it my responsibility to stick by my family through thick and thin and protect our secrets. The events, instead of being about my home environment, would uncoil around my rebellious sixteen-year-old brother, who had a habit of expressing blatant disrespect to our mother. He decided to run away, again, one night and for the first time, I felt he was justified in his doing so.

It was a weeknight and Momma arrived home drunk yet again. Her bar trip cut short this time, whether it was because she ran out of money or couldn't find a man to buy her the drinks. Normally she would leave for her night on the town around 7:00 P.M. and then arrive back home around 5:00 or 6:00 A.M. the following morning. She would come in, put on some coffee and make sure we were up and running to meet the bus for school. On this night she came home early, around 10:00 P.M. and nobody escorted her in.

The etchings of this memory will always be imprinted on me as I recall her sitting in her old burgundy recliner, worn by years. Turning the television on, she told us to run and get showers then get to bed for school, as if she finally decided to be a mother, but the voice was not a loving tone. As she sat there, with the T.V. announcing that evening's news, you could hear her rummaging through her purse. Now our mom was a true woman when it came to her purse. She had all of the receipts from her last month of store trips, including her bills and the envelopes they came in, wallet, makeup, brush, medicines, scissors, address book, etc. You get the picture — the old saying, "everything but the kitchen sink."

She was throwing things at the end table, onto the floor and cursing just about every other word that came out of her mouth. She soon turned her drunken aggression to my brother, Sam. His name was embedded in a barrage of profanity and accusations. She was adamant of the existence of a twenty dollar bill; and even more the accusation that he had removed it from her wallet. She cursed his sheer existence, perverting him as a sorry excuse for a son. Sam and I stood in the hall debating whether to enter the living room area or just turn back to our rooms. I had just exited the bathroom while he was getting ready to go in. We looked at each other in anticipation of what was to come. With all of her ranting and raving, we tried to ignore her, knowing that she was drunk, but Momma seemed angrier than usual and it scared me. At some point, I became so afraid that I went into Sam's room and it obviously concerned him too, because he left the bathroom and followed me, locking the door behind. We sat in his room for only a small moment, thinking that our absence would remove us as being targets of her discontent. But it did not and Sam wore the target.

Realizing she wasn't going to stop screaming at him until he came at her beckoning, he walked down the hall towards the living room. Constant screaming between the two ensued as mother tried to make him admit he had stolen her money.

"You're drunk!" he yelled.

"Where is my dang money you sorry excuse for a son?" she yelled back with curse words instead of those written here.

"You probably drank it away like you always do!" his voice escalating with frustration. He turned and headed back down the hall, his fist clenched close to his side and his jaws clenched even tighter, as if the structure of his jaw bone wasn't strong enough to contain his anger. The stare in his eyes when he got back to the room was so different than anything I had seen before. Momma could be heard following him down the hall, so I shut his door and locked it. She got to the room and began banging on the door, screaming words at him that a mother just doesn't call her own child. He stood almost spaced out as if trying to figure out something. In my mind, I knew there was about to be a huge blow-up, unlike anything we had seen so far, and we had seen many. It broke my heart observing him. I watched as his stare turned back to that of a cold, deep anger. The banging continued at the door. This was it. I knew if something didn't give, Sam was going to be sent back to the detention home, if not arrested and put somewhere more serious; and it wouldn't be fair this time because he didn't start it.

"He didn't take it Momma!" I ran over to and banged at the door, but did not open it. "Go away. You're drunk!" I yelled at her, continuing to pound at the door hoping to scare her. It didn't.

She continued to ignore me and kept taunting him. There were many times when I had to separate the two of them; but this one night all I wanted to do was tuck myself under the bed and pray for it all to go away. Like I said, it was different, everything about it from the fact that she returned home alone and early, to the adjectives she was interjecting into her sentences, mostly entailed with curse words, but more violent and hateful than anytime I ever recalled. Realizing she was just getting angrier at our presence being shut off from her, I contemplated opening the door and trying to reason with her, but the truth is, even I was scared. Momma had hurt me before, but never scared me. So I stood there, no longer banging back, but frozen in shock, awaiting Sam's reaction as my heart pounded faster with each passing second. He didn't move. At some point, she finally quit beating on the door and moved on into her own bedroom, directly catty-cornered from his, with continued cursing under her breath. Who knows why she finally stopped. Maybe she wore herself out, whatever the reason, I was glad. Relief settled within me and I moved my way towards his bed where I sat watching him.

Sam began digging in his closet and my heart tensed even more as my mind raced absurdly with what ifs. What if he is going for that gun? Everything seemed to go silent and Sam slowly turned around with a case in

78

his hand. It seemed like eternity while I registered in my mind the suitcase as luggage and not a rifle case. He threw it onto the bed. His eyes were red and puffy as he tried to fight back the tears. Sam was breathing as if he'd just run a five-mile trek, trying to catch his breath. I knew that he was hurting. Then it happened. Our eyes met and all of the confusion and fear that I had been experiencing washed away from me. My emotions turned to empathy. Sam took the gaze caught between us and very slowly, and through streams of tears and an exasperated breath, asked quietly, "Why does she keep doing this to me?"

My heart ached so heavily for him because for the first time I saw not his defiance—which is what I expected and was accustomed to—but his love. The type of love a child yearns for from their mother. The type of rejection that children feel when they believe they have truly let their mother down. The problem was that this child, Sam, had done nothing. He hadn't stolen her money. She probably drank it away and forgot she'd just come back from a bar. However, the things she had called him on that night could never be taken back. They stabbed at his heart so deep that it wasn't even worth the fight in him to go back at her. He simply wanted to run. It was this time in my life that makes me ponder how many people are hurt so badly by those whom they love that they run from them instead of fight for them. They simply know no way to get through to tell them how much they really love them and want their love in return. We tend to see fighting as a bad thing. Raising our voices, reprimanding those we care about. But if it gives us a chance to express our feelings in an open and honest way, then surely at times it has to be acceptable. Because if it's worth arguing then there must be some sort of hope that we still see in it. I'm not saying it's appropriate to attack those we love, obviously my mother's words on that night were so irreproachable that it removed any shred of hope that Sam held on to.

Sam and I talked about several options. We thought of running away to Florida where he could go shrimping and earn money to provide us with food. There we might possibly hook up with an old friend of his, Captain Timmy, and get a place to live until we could find something else. Experience had also taught Sam that we could stay in a shelter if we needed temporary living—he discovered this the last time he ran away from home. As we talked, it sounded like a good sound plan. I wasn't quite sixteen yet, but I knew Momma was wrong this time, and someone had to watch out for my brother, so I took it upon myself to do just that. As we continued talking and he was completing his suitcase, I went to my room to gather a few necessities. I had to have some basic clothes. Light travel would be ideal for the anticipated walking. I also grabbed my curling iron, a necessity for a teenage girl in the eighties, and my Bible which served as the only true source of peace I'd found in the past seven years. While gathering my stuff together I had time to think about what we were doing…even though it only took a few minutes to scurry through my things and determine what I could and couldn't do without, I had enough time to think.

"Sam, I'm not so sure about running away," I stated.

"Well, you don't have to. But I am getting out of here. I can't take this crap anymore."

"No, I want to go with you, what I mean is running away to Florida. What if we get separated or what if someone picks us up and rapes me?" I asked. This obviously gave him reason to ponder.

"Well, what do you think we should do?" he asked me sincerely.

"I was thinking about the signs — the billboards on Hwy 280. They have a run–away-hotline ad. An 800 number."

"Sis, I can't do that. The state will pick us up and I'll be back in a detention home and I am not going back there," he added.

"Well, what else can we do? At least we will be safe."

"You know, I don't know what you will do, but I can't stay here any longer. Captain Timmy is a sure thing. We just have to get there. And Tammy, I've done it so many times, I know we can do it."

"I just don't know, Sam. I can see where you are fine by yourself but I'm scared of what would happen if a stranger picks us up."

"Crap, Tammy, you're making this hard. It doesn't have to be."

I believe Sam was concerned about the potential issues I raised because he started pacing and didn't speak to me for a little while. It was as if we were stuck in limbo, knowing that we had to do something, but not knowing how to do it. Finally I came up with a sound plan.

"Sam, let's call Sister Maria." Sister Maria, my church pastor, as stated earlier, had become a friend to me. I knew she was a woman of God and that surely of all people she could give us good advice. She might even put us up.

"Okay, call her," he agreed. So I took him up on it before he changed his mind. He had a phone in his room, therefore we didn't have to leave the room and take a chance of Momma overhearing.

After she answered, I filled her in and Sister Maria sympathized with us. After listening intensely to every word I uttered, her pastoral role kicked in and she prayed with me then suggested we call our social worker. She knew of Sam's trouble and could assist us. I went back into my room to gather the social worker's phone number. Thankfully I had learned to trust her and kept her card tucked away just in case I ever needed to talk. After reentering Sam's room, I picked up the phone and began dialing. I called her office number and got an answering machine but it referred me to an emergency phone number to call. I dialed it and then after speaking briefly with an answering service, within just a few minutes we received a call back.

"Hello," came the echo from our end of the phone and on the other end was a woman's voice asking, "May I speak with Tammy?"

"I've got it," I told mother, with my heart racing. I never considered Momma might answer the phone. Momma stayed on the phone for a few more seconds acting like she didn't hear me and that she wasn't there, but I knew better. I finally said in a discouraged voice, "Mom, I've got it. Please hang up, it's for me." With that, she hung up. I heard the click and then proceeded with my call. I filled in our social worker on the details of the night as it unfolded, word by word, including our

82

thoughts of running away and our reason for not doing so. She then asked me what we were going to do.

"We are leaving tonight," I responded. "I just wanted to know if you would come and get us or not. You said if we ever needed you to call. You gave me your card and told me I could call you," I kept saying, afraid she would tell me no.

At that exact moment, Sam spoke up, disrupting the whole plan.

"I'm not going," he said. "Tammy, this isn't right, we can't do this to Mom. Hang up the phone. It's not right! Who will take care of her? She can't help it, you know!"

I sat there stunned for a second time. This time in disbelief and confusion. I just couldn't understand him or my momma anymore and I knew I couldn't handle it. This was my one time that I would be strong enough to leave and if I turned back I knew I would never be this brave again. As I had done so many times on the school bus coming home, I turned my feelings off and as if I had rehearsed it before, I responded in a soft and somewhat defeated voice,

"Please come and get me...Sam isn't coming, but I can't stay here any longer."

My social worker then explained to me that she had to put a few things in order and would be calling me back in just a few minutes, that I was to stay by the phone and answer when she called and to tell Sam that if he changed his mind, that would be alright too. She told me not to worry once we hung up because she would call me right back. As we hung up, I looked at Sam who was staring me down as if I had just betrayed him and

Momma. I couldn't understand how he could go from wanting to run away to wanting to stay and take care of Momma. Looking back, Sam may have been more worried about Ms. Kelley picking us up as she is the one who had taken him to the detention home several times, but I believe he was genuinely hit with the reality that we were leaving our mother and sincerely questioning what would happen to her. Two things played out differently this time for him. One, he had time to think. He didn't just pack his bag and walk out the door to deal with the consequences afterwards. Second, this time I was not staying behind to look out for Momma and deep down inside, we both knew she needed at least one of us.

Before Mrs. Kelly called back, Sam and I had an opportunity to discuss the situation. Informing me about how upset he was that I would follow through with such a thing, he spent at least two solid minutes lecturing me about tearing apart our family. Not affected by his tone or scolding, I let him speak because, as I stated, I had turned my feelings off and simply dealt with him as I had all the other people when they said things that I didn't want to hear. I went into a protective zone where no words could hurt me.

It had not been quite five minutes when the phone rang again. This time before answering I yelled down the hall, "I've got it," and then proceeded with a "Hello," being careful to listen to whether or not Momma was on the other end. No other noises were apparent, so I continued with my call. It was the social worker. She stated that she and a policeman would be coming to my house to pick me up. She assured me to not be scared, explaining that it was standard procedure in case my mother resisted allowing me to go. I asked her not to bring him because he would scare my mother and I didn't want that, it just wouldn't be necessary. Still, she assured me that he wouldn't scare Momma and that she had no option. She had to bring him for her safety; she didn't have a choice. Thinking and agreeing that Ms. Kelley might indeed have reason to worry about her own safety, I finally agreed. She provided me with a detailed time estimate of when to expect them, explained to me how she would approach my momma, assuring me they would not hurt my mother and she would not get in trouble. She then told me what I needed to pack.

After we hung up, I walked into the bathroom to get the rest of my makeup. Mom was finishing up going to the bathroom. In our house, the women didn't have boundaries on how many of us could be in the bathroom at the same time. I looked at Mom and noticed that she looked as if she had had too much to drink. Maybe it wasn't the lack of money that sent her home. Maybe that is why her temper was so volatile, maybe she got evicted. Who knew? It was obvious she was very restless but in that instance, she also looked beautiful — she was, after all, my mother and I didn't know when I would see her again. In spite of all of the things she'd put my brother and me through, Momma spoiled me to the best of her ability. I was her little girl that she always wanted; and everybody that knew us, knew that I was her pride and joy.

There was a strong sense of self-preservation that God graced my body with and on that night in particular, it definitely kicked in. I'm sure all the years of abuse from Momma's boyfriends helped to thicken that self-preservation more than those kids on the school bus.

Regardless, it came in handy that night. I remember how much I hated walking into that bathroom. I knew it would only be conflict and recall our last conversation before I left home.

I said, "Momma, I'm leaving tonight. I can't take this anymore."

She just looked at me through her drunken eyes without a care as to what I'd said.

"I'm serious. Sam didn't take your money. You've got severe problems and I don't want to live here anymore. I just can't!"

Momma laughed at me and said, "Yeah, where are you going?"

I could tell she didn't take me seriously, so I stood firmly by the door, directly staring into her blood-shot eyes and said, "Momma, I'm not kidding. The social worker is coming to pick me up. That was her that called on the phone."

The phone call recollection hit a nerve because at this point, fear built up in her face. Not only fear, but anger too.

"You aren't going anywhere! You are my child and no one is taking you from me!" she said, as she finished her business and started moving towards me. Realizing that for many years now, she had been investigated by the state to have us removed, but always we lied and covered to not be taken from our home. I know that is where the fear was coming from, the reality that it might actually happen.

Carefully, backing out of the bathroom, knowing that it would take her a few moments before she could reach me, I squared myself off again—at the hallway door—and responded.

"Momma, you can't stop me. She's bringing a police officer with her in case you try to stop this. Please Momma, don't. Just let me go. I can't do this anymore." With that, I went to my bedroom quickly and locked the door.

Momma came out of the bathroom yelling for Sam while she was sobbing, demanding him to tell her why this was happening. Sam walked with her into the kitchen, trying to console her. I could hear her puffing and coughing through her cigarette as she was sobbing through her "sorries" with Sam. He came back to my room and knocked on the door, instructing me to let him in. I opened the door very slightly so that he could enter, but making sure Momma was not there, then shut and relocked it behind him. Through his own tears, he asked me why I felt a need to tear apart our family and more specifically why I was hurting Mom in the manner I was.

"She doesn't deserve this," he stated, "Besides, she didn't do anything to you!"

Sitting on my bed, shaking my head in disbelief, the only way I could respond was to laugh. There were no words for the confusion I was going through in my head. I couldn't believe he was talking to me this way. He had started it. He was mad. He saw how she was acting and he was the one who had originally planned to run away. At some point, his speaking turned into a talk full of coarse words about how disrespectful I was being and how I was tearing apart our family. During these words, I emotionally went completely numb. Maybe it had to happen this way so that I could actually walk out the door when the time came. I stood at my window, staring into the night feeling very alone, this time without the tears, just as I had done a lifetime ago, and with a different kind of emptiness, too.

I don't remember much more about that night except Sam leaving my room and the long wait for the social worker and policeman to arrive. When they did, Momma put up a little fight and so did Sam—mostly verbal. But I walked in a straight path, as if I were a robot, to my social worker. She wrapped her arms around me like a blanket shielding me from the cold air of intensity. I'm positive I must have told Momma and Sam that I was sorry and that I loved them but that I had to do this. Yet all I remember is walking out of our front door with Ms. Kelley. Aside from the police car's blue lights, I don't remember anything, not stepping onto the porch or getting into the car. The rest of the night is a blur. I simply remember waking up the next day in a detention home and going downstairs for breakfast. I was only there because I needed somewhere to spend the night. The kids living at the detention center even commented that I didn't belong there.

Isaiah 58:11 (NKJV)
The Lord will guide you continually,
And satisfy your soul in drought,
And strengthen your bones;
You shall be like a watered garden,
And like a spring of water, whose waters do not fail.

A Teacher's Prayer

CHAPTER 8 – New Beginnings

I made a decision that it was time for a new beginning. While I have very little memory of the night I left home after walking out of the door, I woke up the next morning fresh and rapt with a new spirit. I contemplated starting my life afresh, unreservedly accepting this second chance. I changed absolutely everything but my dependence upon God, because I felt that He was the only one I had with me through all of this. I changed my diehard Alabama devotion to War Eagle, only because the act would be a complete opposite and would symbolize the change within me. I reversed my attitude from worrying about what everybody else thought of me to nobody knows me and I'm going to try everything and anything. I also altered my 'favorite' music taste from country to pure rock and roll. Of course there were physical changes, but not as drastic. I changed my hair from long to short before letting it grow out again.

The biggest transformation in my life, however, would come about in school. It was only in small part a shift in attitude and more about what I couldn't change for myself. This alteration did not take place as immediately as the others I 'decided on.' It came from meeting teachers who pushed me; a home staff that supported me, provided me with safety and helped me with my studies; and a window of opportunity in which I finally figured out that I was capable of learning anything if I applied myself and did my homework. It came from a sense of security, and in turn, a willingness to take on more.

Before I left Momma's home, I saw school as a burden, but afterwards it was a gift of knowledge. I wanted to learn everything anyone would teach me. It was the hard-knock lessons that I had learned my whole life; now I was ready for the book lessons. After leaving home, learning was about our country, our religion…it was about opportunity, hope, peace and happiness. If that doesn't motivate someone to grow in knowledge, I don't know what does. This fresh start had to begin somewhere and through that came opportunities that I could choose to take or leave.

Over the span of four months, October through January, I would attend four different schools; have five living arrangements; and begin searching for the person I wanted to become every day. My stay at the detention home was very short-lived. After the first day, Ms. Kelley arranged for me to move into a foster home. I was there for two weeks when I realized it wasn't where I belonged. The foster family was upstanding in the community and in the foster care association, but I had my own opinion after two weeks. Some of the things I observed taking place did not appear ethical for a foster care family. I had enough common sense to know it's not acceptable to "lock" a five year old foster child into a room to play alone because you don't want to watch after her. I also got frustrated at them for constantly yelling at two teenage foster children because they wanted to date another race. This was hard for me to deal with, as the argumentativeness only served as a reminder of what I'd left my own home to get away from. I sure didn't want to be in a similar situation; otherwise I would've stayed at home where I had already learned how to cope.

At this home I saw first hand the waste of money being handed to them for their role as foster parents. I was told that each month they received money to care for each foster child. At the time I was staying there, there were four of us. The money was to be used to provide care for us. To help with the cost of food, clothing, entertainment and personal hygiene care. It probably did not cover all the expenses, but should have helped to provide those types of things.

I was horrified upon returning from school one day, learning that the lady of the house brought in two brown paper bags full of clothes from the Salvation Army Store. She immediately instructed her biological daughter to go through first and pick out what she wanted and then to pass the bag to us girls. My mother, at least, bought me clothes from Wal-Mart or K-Mart, when needed and when able. I assumed the difference of the money was being used to finance the new in-ground pool.

One night while the couple went out to eat, their eighteen year old son was left to watch over us. Certain rules were issued such as our inability to use the phone in their absence. Figuring this to be my only chance to tell Ms. Kelley that I couldn't handle living there, I exaggerated my feelings to their son in order to use the phone. So unsure of all of the change and what exactly what was and wasn't acceptable, I only trusted Ms. Kelley. I needed her to reassure me that things were going to be alright or she would come and get me.

I devised a story and told their son that I was feeling suicidal, asking permission to call my social worker. My advantage was that I'd only been there for two weeks, so he didn't know me well enough to know when I was bluffing. Because cell phones were not readily available to the general public, he was unable to reach his parents to get help, and afraid of what exactly I might do, he allowed me to call Ms. Kelley. Upon reaching her, I very quickly and as quietly as possible, told her that things were very dreadful at the home she placed me in and that if she didn't come and get me I would run away. I told her that I was fearful for them to come home that night and discover that I had called her. I knew they would be furious. I tried to urge her to come and get me immediately, but she didn't. She calmed me down and then explained to me how she would handle the situation. After assuring me that I'd be okay, she then asked to speak with their son, who had been left in charge.

That night when the foster parents got home there was a note for them to call Ms. Kelley. She explained to them that I'd had a very bad day emotionally. She continued to tell them about the changes I was going through and how she would be driving out the next day, Sunday, to visit with me and take me for a walk where we could talk. She asked them not to mention anything at all about the conversation to me. I learned all of this the next day while she and I were on our walk.

I will always wonder what was going through her mind. Did she believe me, about my perception of this family, on the phone? I surely convinced her after she got there, because I had no clue that she was going to have me pack that very day and take me with her when she left. Because of her decisive reaction and trust of me, she probably saved me from more pain and for that I will be forever grateful. Since that time, I have heard of many great foster stories where families provide a loving and honest home life for children in need. I am so proud to support them in any way possible in my community today. I have heard and met many amazing foster families and I know the difference they can make for a child. Unfortunately, it just wasn't my personal experience, yet I now know that God had other plans for my life.

After leaving the foster home, I headed back to the Detention Center for another night. I recall absolutely nothing about that stay. I only spent one more night there and then was sent to the Emergency Shelter in Sylacauga, Alabama. The transition to the Shelter is an empty memory, but I have plenty of remembrances while living there; although it only lasted for a few months. It was a temporary stay while the state searched for a permanent residence for me.

I had been there for a little over a month when Ms. Kelley called me to tell me the good news. At the end of December I would be moving to the King's Ranch in Oneonta, but could only remain there for one year. She advised me that I would be required to move away for a short time because of state funding requirements. She then explained how, after a certain period of time passed, I'd be able to return again if I chose. I wasn't scared about the Kings Ranch. I'd already moved three times and handled it fairly well. I counted on the fact that if I could make it through walking out the front door of my momma's house then I could do anything; not that I wanted to move again. Yet I was game for anything at that point in my life. And I only had to make it to sixteen and then I could make my own calls, or so I thought. My goals were still to quit school and begin taking care of myself.

A Teacher's Prayer

Romans 8:28 (NIV)
*And we know that all things work together for good
to those who love God,
to those who are the called according to His purpose.*

CHAPTER 9 – Emergency Shelter

It was after leaving the foster family and spending another night in the detention home, that I would move to find some short-term consistency. My social worker explained to me about a group home that was an emergency shelter, where her agency had placed many children who were in transition. Since I would not move to the King's Ranch until January, being in this place would allow me to rest my head for the time leading up to the move. During the few months I resided at the Shelter, I became very comfortable there. The ladies, known as houseparents, were incredibly kind and compassionate. In fact, they mothered me to death, so to speak. Since the night I had left home, I had not spoken with my mother. Ms. Kelley probably did; I'm not sure. But I made the decision not to call my mother and nobody pushed me to do it either. I arrived at the Shelter approximately two weeks after I ran away from home.

At the onset, I did not contact my mother, for I knew that I wasn't strong enough to talk to her without wanting to go running back. I knew she missed me, but I wasn't ready. My fear was that her neediness would creep back into guilt and that would drive me home to her. As long as we didn't talk, I could shut out that confusion for the time. Somehow, I knew this beyond a shadow of a doubt; so I simply didn't call until I was confident of my ability to handle it.

Living at the Shelter had its moments. There were kids there in transition, moving to a larger group home like I was. There were children who were taken away from their parents, but didn't behave well enough to stay in foster care, yet misbehaving badly enough to be placed in a detention center. There were children who were living there temporarily until the courts could grant custody to some type of family member. I was somewhere in between.

The Shelter was a very impressionable place—so picturesque. A huge horseshoe drive, semi-circles in the front of the two-story colonial- style home. It is housed on approximately three acres of beautifully kept wooded land with some clearing in the front and to the side. When walking into the front double doors, you enter into a massive room which includes, to the right, a living room area with a large TV, a couple of sofas and a few chairs, all circling around a big throw rug in the middle of the arrangement. To the left was a dining area with a large table seated with twelve chairs and a huge china cabinet that shelved everyday dishes and a few vases and trinkets. Straight ahead was an island that separated the kitchen. It was the largest kitchen I had ever seen. The Shelter was decorated so beautifully…it reminded me of the house on the old TV sitcom The Facts of Life. Ironic, because at the time I didn't recall the prayer, but would before too long.

Living in the group home setting was like living with a whole bunch of brothers and sisters. It wasn't The Facts of Life at all. In that show, they were all girls and around the same age. In the Shelter, we were all different ages, sexes, and races. There were kids I was close to and those whom I couldn't stand to be in the room with. As in the sitcom, the houseparents were, by far, dearest to me. They were very giving of their time and care for us. We always had clean sheets on our beds, a wonderful assortment of food for every meal, nice clothes and all of the personal hygiene items a child could want.

Off to the left of the kitchen was a hall that led to some of the offices and houseparent rooms, as well as an opening to a corridor which led to the activity room. This was a large room which resembled an old fellowship hall at a church. It appeared to have been a separate building at one time, probably a garage that had been converted when the home was turned into an emergency Shelter. This was a fun room with jump ropes, large balls and a huge open floor where we were allowed to run wild if we wanted. Mostly the smaller children, ages four to ten, would spend their time in here. Off to the right of the living room was a staircase that led upstairs to the girls' rooms. The steps stretched up two flights before entering a large hall. At the cap of the steps was a bathroom with two stalls and two showers. To the left was one bedroom, while to the right of the bath were two others. On the left, in the large room is where Kristi and I (both of us in tenth grade) shared two sets of bunk beds. It was beautiful, with lots of windows and a fire exit to the outside.

Kristi and I developed a friendship immediately. She had gorgeous red hair and was very thin, like I was, but she knew how to care for hair and makeup. She dressed in the prettiest of clothes. She appeared to be a very nice person and quite funny to be around as long as she wasn't in a bad mood. We got along very well, with one exception. She wasn't into the Bible and didn't understand why I read it all the time. Looking back, I'm sure I read it for the peace, but it was the only consistency I had in my life at that time. I couldn't have possibly explained it to her if the opportunity did arise. It didn't come between us though. I really didn't discuss God with her at all, probably because our relationship was too short-lived. Our time talking was consumed by school and guys. Considering we only lived together for a month, we got away with this being the gist of our conversations. Kristi was wild. She taught me a lot of tricks of the trade that I would've never thought of on my own. Unfortunately, she also had a lot of problems at home and while I don't recall knowing why she was at the Shelter, I believe she was also under the care of the state.

Kristi was the first to teach me a thing or two about cosmetology. When it came to makeup, she was impressive. Her pale, freckled skin and blue eyes, with long black lashes looked absolutely lovely with her translucent face powder and rose pink blush. Her makeup didn't cover up her temper though. When she got angry her whole face turned the color of her hair — red!

One of the most memorable moments with her wasn't long after I started to the local public high school. She'd already been attending for a month or so when I came, so she took it upon herself to take me under her wing and show me around. I don't think a good mother would've approved of the type of things she showed me, but I was by myself and if this is where I could belong then it was worth exploring. I hadn't been at the Shelter for even two weeks when she introduced me to a secret. After arriving home from school, we ate dinner, helped wash the dishes and then wandered up to the rooms where we began giggling the night away. It must have been the giggling that caused us to finally bond, because that night she asked me to sneak out with her. She had repeated this feat several times to meet up with her boyfriend. The actual incentive seemed to be that he was sixteen and had a car. They had planned to meet this particular evening around 11:00 and she wanted to know if I would go with her. I laughed at her because I knew she was wild. But crazy? How in the world did she think she was going to sneak out without getting caught, and more importantly, what if she did get caught?

I only thought I was *thinking* these things, but as it turned out, I said them out loud.

She then laughed at me and said, "Tammy, I've been in and out of so many group homes. The worst is that we will get picked up by the police and be brought back here."

The thought made my stomach turn. I was not the type to get into trouble for fun. It occurred only out of reacting, not planning.

"The fact is," she stated, "I've been doing this for a while here. You see, we have the best room in the house. See this fire alarm? On the other side of this exit door is a stairway leading down to the ground. I rigged the alarm and it won't go off."

By this time my nervousness was replaced with curiosity and intrigue, so I encouraged her to go on. How in the world did she rig it? She refused to tell me her secret, but I would later discover that she'd clogged up the alarm with toothpaste, smothering the sound. I was in, and now I just wanted to do it for the sheer dare of it…wondering if it really would work.

That night, Mama Flo (one of our houseparents) came up and tucked us in tight. She said a prayer with us and then walked back down the stairs as she had done routinely each night that she worked. She was my favorite houseparent and when she gave me her nightly hug I felt a small hint of deception overwhelm my conscience. However, when 11:00 P.M. came, afraid I would appear to be a chicken if I backed out, I was up and dressed, ready to try it. I may have been a Bible reader / believer, but I was still a teenage girl and I couldn't wait to see if it really worked. Boy, just wanting to know if you're going to be able to get away with something will more times than not override your good conscience and I learned to be careful with this.

Kristi was right. We successfully made it out and back in, without detection on that night. As we took off running down the highway, each time a headlight could be seen coming our way, we would dive into the ditches. My heart would race from pure fear. One, I was scared of getting caught and getting in trouble. Two, I was scared of getting picked up by someone we definitely didn't want to get picked up by — like some man without any respect for a teenage girl. Third, and most importantly, nagging at me, what was the point of getting dressed up to meet guys if you are only going to roll in grass with dew, dirt and rocks? My sneaking out days with Kristi were over, but it wouldn't have lasted much longer anyway. Shortly after that night she was picked up by the police while attempting another sneak out. She was correct in knowing that the police might pick her up, but she was very wrong about where they would take her. I'm not sure where she went because we children weren't told. She didn't return. Mama Flo packed her things while we were at school.

Mama Flo was precious. She had short, curly dark brown hair with a hint of gray in it. She was a very well-dressed lady with glasses and yet another who knew just how to apply her makeup. She was also a good Christian woman. Not long after Kristi left us, Mama Flo came up to talk to me about how sometimes friends come and go in our lives, but we should always give thanks to God for them. How each person we encounter has a special purpose for entering our lives at that time, whether it is a lesson for them to learn or one for us. Someone, maybe even both, will benefit from the relationship. This was also the night that she brought me a very special present. She knew I read my Bible every night. Mine was small and worn out. I carefully tore the wrapping paper open on her gift. Whether it was just simply being respectful to receiving a gift from her or wanting to savor the moment, I'm not sure. But inside that unassuming wrapping was a remarkable big book called *The Open Study Bible*. It provided historical facts regarding the authors and times of the various books of the Bible. It also referenced certain verses to others. It was, by far, the coolest Bible I'd ever seen.

The Bible I already had was one I had just happened on a few months before I left home. Momma was so angry at Dad for dying on her that she would constantly tell us both good and bad things about him. I know now how badly she must have hurt and I know this is why she and Sam had so much trouble. Grandma always told me that my brother not only looked like Dad, but acted like him. Sam, being the rebel he was, broke into an Army crate that Mom had sealed off when we left Iowa in 1977. It held some of my father's personal belongings and when Sam and I were old enough, Momma was going to open it up and divvy the things up between us. Sam wasn't able to wait, especially since he liked to run away —

so one day he broke it open. I don't recall the contents which he took, but I got a ceramic bowl that Dad used as his dish when he was a child. I also received Dad's Bible. I was so excited to find it because Momma somehow had me believing Dad went to Hell. That he was a drunk. Grandma always tried to tell me that Momma was just really hurt and wasn't being truthful, but I'd always thought Grandma was being just that—a grandma—and trying to protect us. Not long after I left home, I realized that not only did Grandma tell me the truth about how angry Momma was at my brother for Dad dying, but also why Sam had the problems he had with her treating him so badly. But Grandma was also telling the truth about Daddy too. Many times, reading that Bible, I would miss my brother greatly. I was just too afraid to call him because I didn't want to talk to Momma. I was also afraid he would nag me about coming home, as much as, or more than, Momma. Instead, I would open the Bible every night and read. It was my communication to God. I knew He would watch over my mother and brother and this gave me peace from worrying about them. I put my energies into focusing on getting my life together, but it would prove to be very challenging because I started realizing what a tiny amount I knew about the world in which I lived.

Upon moving into the Shelter, I got to pick out some nice new clothes. While only a handful, they were still very welcomingly received. I also got to go to the supply closet and pick out a new hairbrush, hairspray, toothbrush, toothpaste, shampoo, conditioner and soap. Anything I needed: cotton balls, *Q tips*… I could whatever I needed and didn't have to pay for it. It was one of the oddest, but most exciting firsts I had enjoyed. Who knew my dependency for *Q tips* would become so vital to my cosmetic needs.

The first time I picked out supplies, they literally had to hand them to me because I didn't feel right taking them. I didn't have any money to give for them and Momma taught us not to take things from others, unless she okayed it. It really was a 'pride' thing and an offensive gesture if we were handed items for free. In our family, we didn't accept handouts. After a few visits to the supply closet, I became used to the process of selecting supplies and began looking forward to it. Another thing that was a first was the opportunity to participate in sports. The sports took place at the Shelter, but it was still fun. It wasn't like backyard football with the neighborhood guys. There was an assortment of activities always going on.

Our activities director, Miss Janie, was a recent college graduate and somewhat of a tomboy, but a very pretty girl whose appearance impressed me greatly. She was young, dressed nicely, and had a great haircut. She would come over several times a week and coordinate some sort of activity with us kids. Whether it was playing basketball, football or whatever, she always came up with good ideas and she had a ton of energy to carry it out with us. After about a month, I got to know Janie a little better. She was, in fact, closer to my age than anyone else there that I wanted to hang out with. I don't think I ever told her, but I looked up to her. I thought she was the absolute coolest to come and spend time with us because we all knew those old ladies weren't going to play football with us. Shockingly enough though, they did get out there on occasion.

A Teacher's Prayer

One day Janie did our devotion for us and began telling us a story that made all of our mouths hit the floor. Janie told us that she grew up in a group home just like we were doing. She grew up in the Presbyterian Home for Children, which was actually the parent facility to the Emergency Shelter. I couldn't believe it. She looked and acted so normal. She reminded me of the popular kids at my home high school. She was pretty, fun and had lots of personality—so much that you couldn't have imagined anyone not liking her. She was a college graduate even! *Was her background similar to mine? How did she make it out of this lifestyle to the one she was presenting? Did she have to move all the time? If she lived in a group home, how did she graduate from college?* I had so many questions. She didn't get into a lot of detail about why she was there and I really don't remember the rest of the story of her living there. I just remember that after we got through playing that day, I had to know more. I have never been accused of being shy. In fact, my mouth was responsible for most of my trouble. My mother taught me that I had a voice and it was just as important as anyone else's. Unfortunately, I never learned the political astuteness to using that voice. It didn't always harm me though. Mostly, if I had something to say, I didn't shy away from it. So, I went up to Janie and we talked.

She was so kind. We connected on a different level that day. She could tell I was horribly confused about what "living in a group home" meant. She began to share stories with me of the wonderful place where she grew up. It was a home where she lived with many other kids. She told me that she went to a good public high school and was able to participate in sports or band—it was her

104

choice. They had employees who worked at the home who would drive her to and from the activities, so she was able to get involved at school. She continued to tell me that she had similar living arrangements as we did at the Shelter. However, because there were so many children they were divided up by age groups into separate cottages, similar to dormitories at colleges. She filled me in on their basketball team and Olympic size pool. Most importantly, she told me that she didn't have to move around. She had lived there for several years. They helped her to go on to college where she eventually graduated.

I couldn't believe it. In the past month, I'd already moved four times with no real permanence in sight. It just sounded too good to be true. So, I asked her how she got there. I don't remember her answer, but somehow it triggered me to call Ms. Kelley again and tell her about the home I'd discovered. Isn't it absolutely amazing about what Mama Flo said about God's purpose in bringing people together? Here I was, scheduled to go to the King's Ranch in one more month, but I could only stay there for a year. While my life had been quite exciting and full of adventure in the two months since I had left home, I definitely wouldn't have minded being still for a while. This was the first time I had ever considered going to college and it was a surreal thought. My whole teenage life to this point was about turning sixteen and leaving high school. Now I wanted to actually consider grad-uating high school. Could it even be possible to go to college too? My grades had been mediocre at best. Did I have what it takes?

Ms. Kelley called back within a few days after our conversation. She told me that I could have an oppor-

A Teacher's Prayer

tunity to go to the Home if I really wanted to. She would set up an appointment, take me out to visit it first and if I decided I liked it, then we would get in touch with my mom. This would be necessary because the Home was not operated by the State so my mother would have to give them permission to keep me. My stomach knotted up. All of the hopes I had been enjoying since talking with Janie faded quickly away. I knew there wasn't any way that my mom was going to give up her little girl.

She didn't want to let me go on that night. Did Ms. Kelley really think she would sign me over to someone else? Who in the world was she kidding and more importantly, who did she think she was talking to? Maybe she didn't know me and my situation as much as I thought she did. I hung up the phone very dejected. Before we said good-bye though, Ms. Kelly recognized my disappointment and told me she would give me time to think about it. She knew I hadn't yet spoken with Mom and that I should take some time to decide if I was ready to do so. Once again, God and I had a long talk that night. I was desperately pleading with God because all hope seemed to be fading.

During those long prayers and after a night of good sleep, I awoke to a new-found peace. I had made up my mind. It couldn't hurt to try, but definitely would hurt to *not* try. This is when the word and actions of opportunity in a positive way began to take root in my life; because I understood that not trying would possibly cause me to lose out on something I longed for. That day, after school, I called Ms. Kelley who set up an appointment and took me out to visit the Home. It was after Thanksgiving.

The leaves had fallen from the trees and a cool breeze embraced the historical city of Talladega, Alabama.

A Teacher's Prayer

The campus was located on approximately fifteen acres with twelve or thirteen beautiful light red brick buildings situated in a pattern that seemed to surround itself. Back from the main road was one building sitting off by itself with a beautiful walkway, lined with flower beds running on either side and including a circular collection in the middle. Directly across from it, past the road, was a large, brick patio area that housed a huge dining hall. It was centered in the middle, utilizing steps which led off to two brick office buildings connected by the walkway on each side. Off to the right of this section sat a two story cottage, which I later came to know as Johnson Cottage or Independent Living. I found out it was a place where the teenage boys and girls lived. They had to be at least a junior in high school and had to go through an application process to be admitted. On the left were two more brick homes, known as cottages. They housed different age groups of boys—pre-teens and teens (not quite ready to move into Johnson Cottage). Behind the dining hall was a chapel, a gymnasium, an Olympic size swimming pool and another two-story cottage where the social workers, chaplain and some houseparents resided. Back even further were four more cottages—each single story. Also located in the back was the President's home.

Of the four cottages, there was one coed for very small children (ages 3-7); there was one for pre-teen girls, one for teenage girls and one for little boys, named Abbey Cottage, Mohns Cottage, Jordan Cottage and Robinson Cottage, respectively. There was a playground between the young children's cottage and the adult cottage. There were basketball courts dispersed throughout the campus and a big red barn back beyond Robinson.

A Teacher's Prayer

It was apparent to me, after meeting the staff as well as some of the children, that I would be calling my mother. I was terrified. Ms. Kelley and I discussed my options while driving back to the Shelter. She agreed with me that it sounded like a nice place for a child to live. Ms. Kelley explained that it would have to be my decision as to whether or not she should call my mother and ask. I was stunned. I never thought of the possibility of Ms. Kelley calling Mother and that started to lighten my nerves up somewhat; until I remembered who we were talking about. I knew Mother had to have the most awful grudge against Ms. Kelley for taking her little girl away. I knew if this was something I really wanted it would be up to me to make the contact to ask my mother to place me there. I had time to contemplate what to do. Ms. Kelley was patient with me and did not require an immediate answer. I prayed to God to give me the strength of Samuel, inwardly, and the Wisdom of Solomon.

Philippians 4:13 (NKJV)
I can do all things through Christ who strengthens me.

Chapter 10 – Time to Call

Without rehearsal of the conversation I would have with my mother, just the knowledge and anticipation of such, I began growing resolve in my ability to follow through. While it took a couple of days to finally decide I would be okay making the call, I eventually found a sense of calm which enabled me to go forward. Momma Flo was on the couch reading when I descended the stairs. Walking over to join her in the living room, I sat down beside her. Peering over her book towards me, she let silence fill the air.

"I'm ready to call my mother," I offered.

Patting me on the shoulder, she gave me a reassuring smile then led me to the kitchen where she punched in the long distance code before handing me the receiver. As if sensing my confidence, she moved to the outside of the kitchen, yet stayed within hearing distance.

The Shelter was decorated for Christmas so there was an automatic peace about the atmosphere that night. Picking up the phone, I began dialing our number I had memorized while filling out all my paperwork for school: 1-2-0-5-6-9-9-7-2-0-5. It rang two or three times. As I stood there wondering whether or not the phone was still in service, it felt like eternity and I had enough time to begin running scenarios through my head. *The phone was disconnected. Mom moved back to Iowa. Mom was out to a bar. Mom had the TV too loud and didn't hear the phone.* My thoughts were finally interrupted.

"Hello?"

"Hello, Ma-ma?" There was a silent pause which lasted for a few seconds. And my breath escaped me momentarily. *Momma!* I cried out in my head before her response interrupted me.

"Tammy?" Mom asked.

"Yes ma'am," I answered, thrilled to be speaking to her, to know she was okay, but reminding myself of the importance of being strong.

"Tammy! Tammy, oh baby, how are you?" she said as tears begin to sob on the other side.

"Mom, I'm fine," I responded. "How are you?" My emotions shut down again as she barraged me with a million questions.

"Oh, Tammy honey, I'm wonderful now. Are you okay? Are you hurt? What's wrong, honey? I've missed you so much!"

In her good ole Southern drawl, through what seemed like endless questions, she finally stopped long enough to allow me to respond. I'm one hundred percent sure these are the kind of questions any good mother would ask of her child that walked out the door one night unexpectedly and then didn't call for the following two months. Strangely enough though, I didn't get rattled by her tears. The empathy I had felt over all of those years for her was pushed aside early in the call because I knew I had a task at hand which had to get done. In my mind I had resolved to be compassionate because I knew I needed her on my side; yet there was a toughness — a wall — that was still standing strong, and for the meantime, I was hiding behind it. I knew if I let myself start caring beyond pretense that I would crumble because I loved my mother and I missed her so much. What I would come to discover though is my underestimation of her 'true love' for me. I briefly told Mom where I was currently living and how I

110

had moved around to several different places including the story of the foster family which I leaned on to play to her maternal instincts. I explained to her of how the constant moving was wearing on me. I told her about how nice everyone had been to me, including the good food that I had been fed and the nice clothes which they'd provided to me. She very patiently listened to my brief but detailed explanation of my whereabouts and then responded with what came as a complete shock to me.

"I'm glad, honey! I'm so sorry if I hurt you and I miss you very much. I want you to come home."

Oh, no! She said it. All of a sudden the wall wasn't solid — more like built on sand. Completely caught off guard by her apology, I found myself speechless and trying to regroup my purpose of the call. Then my mind played through the last part of her dialogue, *"I want you to come home."* Those words were all it took to raise all guards back up and fast. I had nothing else to say because what could I? If I said, "No," she wouldn't give me what I wanted. If I said "I miss you too and want to come home," even though knowing it to be a lie, if spoken, I might actually believe it. I knew I couldn't go home; I just couldn't bare all of that pain again. I had learned about how wrong some of the things that had happened to me truly were. I just wasn't ready to give up my new adventure. I was seeing things in my life that I didn't know were possible. I wasn't afraid of being "at home," anymore.

So silence prevailed. I do recall telling Mom that I loved her and that I missed her, but I didn't apologize for leaving, nor did I feel remorseful for that decision. In fact, I quickly changed the conversation to updating her on making good grades in school and that is when it happened. We'd been on the phone not even five minutes and silence prevailed. The awkwardness seemed to open the perfect window of opportunity for the pivotal question. *My mouth and the trouble it gets me into.* No cordial soft openings, I just dove right in, straight to her heart.

"Momma, I don't want to come back home. Things that happened at home shouldn't have happened and I don't want to come back. I found this place in Talladega where I can go and live while I go to college and I won't have to move any more. I'm tired of moving and I really want to go there. It's a beautiful place and if you saw it, I know you would like it."

No response was heard on the other end. *Maybe I didn't give her time,* I thought to myself.

"Momma, I need your help."

The line was still mostly silent, but I heard her sniffle just a little and then take a very deep breath.

"Momma, I can't go there unless you sign me in." My voice was surely pleading in obvious desperation for her cooperation.

Then I heard her response in a cold spoken language that I had learned to use to communicate with the kids on the bus. It was the kind of conversation that gives an answer someone wants to hear but has a twist of nasty sarcasm on it. That was the voice she used to say,

"Sure, Tammy, if that's what you want."

"It is, Momma; it's a great place and it's what I feel I have to do right now in my life."

"Tammy, I just want you to come home." And with that her stern voice dropped and she continued, "Honey, if you will not come home then I just want you to be somewhere you will be safe and happy. It sounds like a nice place and I would like to come out there and see it with you."

What should have been a moment of happiness turned into painful defeat. *She wants to see it?* My heart sank. I'd prepared to talk to her on the phone, but to see her? *Oh boy, now what was I to do?* I had a feeling deep down in the pit of my stomach that seeing her would be the end to all ends. I would want to go running back home, as soon as I could see how sad and lonely she was without me. I would fall victim to her old ways and responsibilities of family taking care of family. Yet I knew there was no other option and again the opportunity was there and the only way to know was to try. *What else is there to do, Tammy, do you want to go or not? What's it worth?*

So, determined and with a strong voice I answered, "Okay, Momma, we will go see it together but I'm not coming home, do you understand this?"

"Tammy, please, let's just go see it and then we'll decide. I won't take it away from you, if it's really what you want, honey, but I want to see you. I love you."

Even though I was scared, I knew that her words were sincere. I wasn't so much scared of her taking it away from me; I was scared of me running from it straight back into her arms and her home and the life I left behind. The phone call ended shortly after her last comment with the normal 'I love you(s)' and her reminding me, one more time, just how much she missed me. I could feel that I was becoming emotional so I told her I was out of time and had to get off the phone. She begged me to call again as we hung up. That night I went up to my room and cried while cradling myself on the bed, having yet another "comfort" talk with God. I thanked Him that Momma sounded good. I also questioned whether or not I was doing the right thing. Maybe I had no right to decide to take my momma's little girl away from her. God must have been listening because Momma Flo slid into my bed right at that exact moment and wrapped her big, warm, wonderful arms around me. She told me that I was a very brave girl and that she knew it was going to work out the way God intended it to. Sobs began to flow in both of us. I don't know how long we stayed like that. At some point, we finally ended the crying session and she tucked me in bed before praying for me that night.

The next day I awoke and very quickly got back into the swing of things. I didn't perceive it as a choice. I had learned to get up and start each day over anew; because I couldn't have mentally handled it any other way. Sure, I was pushing feelings back deep down inside, but I had learned how to be happy and I really liked that feeling. Here started another day and the best part was, it was the last day of school before Christmas vacation.

Romans 8:26 (NKJV)
Likewise the Spirit also helps in our weaknesses.
For we do not know what we should pray for as we ought, but the Spirit Himself makes intercession for us with groanings which cannot be uttered.

CHAPTER 11– Generosity of Teachers

I had been attending B.B. Comer School for almost a month by the time Christmas rolled around. The kids were cordial, which was new for me to find in a school. I had begun hanging out with Kristi's friends, watching them smoke outside and flirting with the boys between classes, but Kristi was no longer at the school since the night she didn't return from sneaking out. The teachers were also nice and I felt like this was a place I could fit in if I had too. The day before Christmas break was a short one, so not much would be happening, but goofing off centered around a sense of freedom rarely felt in school. One could peg it down to two times a year, really: Christmas break and summer break.

Around 11:30 A.M. I was paged over the intercom to the office and my teacher sent me down the hall to find out why. Of course the dreaded walk to the principal's office had become a memory since leaving home, yet once the walk started, fear crept into me and my gut wrenched at the thought of what I might have done this time. *I was being good now. I was trying. How in the world does trouble seem to follow me?* It had been a while since I snuck out and couldn't think of any trouble I had gotten into recently. *"Kristi was gone and since I had not been hanging outside the school smoking cigarettes... Who knows... I have a knack for office trips?"* I thought to myself. As I walked, I spotted several of the faculty members standing by the teacher's lounge staring at me. With smiles adorning their faces, they intently watched me walk, not once taking their eyes off of me as if in anticipation of something I was supposed to do, or was at least going to do. One of my teachers, but I don't recall which one, called me over to the lounge.

"Tammy, can you please come in here with me for a moment? We have something we want to give you," she said.

Glad that this was the reason I had been paged and not a true visit to the principal, I accepted the invitation and turned to enter the room with them. This was so out of the normal that I couldn't even imagine what was going on, but curiosity drove me forward. I figured they knew I would be leaving the Shelter before school got back into session, so who knew what in the world they could possibly need from me. At this public school in Sylacauga I had begun to form a new habit, befriending my teachers.

As soon as I walked up to my teacher, who had a very inviting hand gesture to come closer, the school bell went off signaling the end to the day and the beginning of the holidays. I stopped in my tracks, wondering what to do because I knew I couldn't miss the bus. My teacher noticed my hesitation and told me not to worry that Ms. Janie from the Shelter would be coming by to pick me up that day.

Walking through the door an outburst of voices echoed "SURPRISE!" In front of me waited a line of teachers clapping and leading me to a table nearby. Stacked on it were presents of all sizes, neatly wrapped, a few with bows and some in gift bags. A flurry of thoughts entered my mind to make sense of the scene. *Maybe the gifts are for all the kids at the Shelter*, I thought. But there were no other kids there from the Shelter, so that ruled out most of my explanations. Did all of these gifts come from the teachers? I had never seen so many except maybe on a

116

television show and I wasn't even sure of that. I had no idea what to say or do.

I continued following the line of teachers motioning me to walk towards the table. After the realization sunk in that they were indeed for me and that the applause was still sounding, I found myself becoming angry. The anger was very temporary and quickly turned to embarrassment as I realized all of the students walking by were peeking in to see what the noise was all about. The very same students that knew Tammy Mentzer didn't have a family and didn't have a house now would know I didn't have anyone to spend Christmas with. I found myself miserable inside...I was so upset at those teachers, questioning how they could do this in front of everybody. I know my face must have turned red and I wonder if they read the humiliation that was surely written all over me. Yet the manners my mother instilled in me offset the pride she had also sworn me to. Accepting defeat of the independence to which I had held so tightly, I walked over to open the gifts, telling myself the whole time, *Tammy, be thankful. They're only being kind. They aren't trying to embarrass you.* At that point, enjoyment was completely gone as I began battling within myself as to why I was acting so badly. *This was indeed a very kind gesture. I knew it was because Momma brought us up to be very independent, not to accept help from others; that we would always take care of each other.* But my family wasn't here to take care of me. In my family, there was a sense of shame to accepting handouts and it was affecting me immensely on this particular day. It's amazing how some things taught to us, with good intentions drive our emotions the wrong way. As the students finally started clearing off the school

117

grounds, I felt more at ease with each opening, but still not happy. Putting on a front for them, I faked my smile, said 'thank you' with each gift opened, hoping to hide the shame I was actually feeling inside.

Some of the surprises that I opened included: a beautiful jewelry box, art supplies, a Bible, a very pretty thin gold necklace with a heart on the end, bracelets, Lisa Frank stationary, makeup and what seemed like a lot of clothes (anything from socks to sweaters). One of the gifts was a London Fog jacket. I didn't know what that meant at the time, but it didn't take Momma Flo long to explain the value of it to me and what a lucky girl I was to have received such a generous gift. I also received a fifty dollar gift certificate to a local department store where I later bought a pair of Guess Jeans and a beautiful sweater. I would've never spent twenty dollars on one outfit when I lived at home, let alone fifty; but it wasn't hard once I was given the opportunity.

The teachers were so thoughtful on that day and while I told them thank you, I know my expression and attitude didn't show gratitude. I truly hope they somehow knew that in a couple of days I became very aware and grateful for what they'd done.

When I returned to the Shelter, my safety zone where I knew I could tell Momma Flo anything, I was spitting mad as I told Mama Flo about what had happened, asking her why they would embarrass me in such a way, assuring her that the Shelter was taking care of me and somebody should've told them that. My voice became more flustered as I asked Momma Flo why they didn't tell them that they were taking care of me and I didn't need anything. Momma Flo, in her loving, patient, non-judgmental way, began to explain to me that they were told I only came with three outfits, very little personal hygiene stuff and one Bible. They knew I would not be returning when school resumed and that I had touched their lives just by coming to their school and they wanted me to know they wished me a wonderful future. She said that they wanted to give me a very special Christmas that I would never forget and to wish me luck in my life that was ahead of me. It was then I began to cry, knowing how selfish and ungrateful I had been, and that night when I talked to God, I blessed those teachers so many times, that surely the angels couldn't hold it all.

2 Corinthians 1:3-5 (NKJV)
Blessed be the God and Father of our Lord Jesus Christ, the Father of mercies and God of all comfort, who comforts us in all our tribulation, that we may be able to comfort those who are in any trouble, with the comfort with which we ourselves are comforted by God. For as the sufferings of Christ abound in us, so our consolation also abounds through Christ.

CHAPTER 12 – Custodial Rights

During the Christmas holidays, Ms. Kelley called the Shelter to speak with me. She wanted me to know that Mom had agreed to set up a time for them to go look at the Presbyterian Home for Children. Ms. Kelley had obviously been updated on the phone call that I had with my mom because she knew I didn't want to accompany them and therefore had arranged to take Mom up there without me. Thank God, my mother agreed to do it.

It was Christmas week when we got the good news; Mom had completed the application and the Home had an opening for a teenage girl. I would be moving there at the beginning of the New Year. With the assurance of moving into the Home, and knowing it could be a more permanent situation, I found an inner peace to go visit with my mother. I almost felt like I owed her for agreeing to it. Knowing it was hard for her to sign me away to the Home, especially not having seen me since I left her, meant as much to me as anything could have in my attempt to make amends.

Ms. Kelley took me to visit Mom that December. Emotionally I was still protected within the walls I had built up, so the memories are few, but I do recall her Christmas gift. I had bought some hand-crafted dish towels for her kitchen. It wasn't unusual for me to mow lawns to make a few bucks or charge my friends initiation fees to clubs. During the summer prior to leaving home, I used some of that money to buy her gift. During our visit, I would discover that she went through all of my things and found it—already wrapped for Christmas. It was in the top right corner of my closet. In fact, she not only found it, but opened it and had been using it since. My brother later told me that finding the gift was very painful for her. That, of all things, was the most emotionally connected feeling I had during that visit. The visit was psychologically draining and it would be several months before I would see my mother again.

In the meantime, Mom and I began regular correspondence, some by letter, and some by phone. I learned to develop a different kind of respect for my mother, understanding that she cared enough about me to allow me to be happy and safe. She did so by accepting my resolve to not return to her. So now I could call her my mother, or simply, 'Mom.' Being at the Home and growing accustomed to the environment, I wanted to ensure that my mother would not deny me the opportunity to stay there.

After moving to the Children's Home, I would develop a deep kind of love through my relationship with Momma Flo—one that included trust. It was so different from anything I had ever felt to that point in my life that saying good-bye to her was one of the hardest good-byes I had ever said. I wanted her to come with me because she had become my crutch for strength and reasoning. Somehow she always knew how and more importantly, when, to say something to me. She knew when she needed to listen and when she needed to explain. Good ole Momma Flo made sure to keep my spirits up and with vigilant strength. She assured me that we would meet time and time again, and we did. She was truly my 'Mama Flo'.

Arriving at the Home in January of 1987, I would encounter many more people, whom I would come to love in a similar way. The Home would start helping me find purpose for myself and set goals for the years ahead, including going to college. Granted, I still didn't have a clue of how to do my makeup or hair once I arrived, but there was time for me to grow in all areas.

Ms. Span, my social worker at the Home, took a special interest in me. I am sure she did with everyone, but she just had a way of making you believe it was just about you. She was a beautiful, energetic and sassy (or confident) lady. Very prim and proper yet very fun-loving; and it was always such a pleasure to be around her. I think one of the things I respected the most about Ms. Span was that she always told me everything just like it was. If we talked about the things that happened to me at home, not only did she tell me it was wrong, but explained to me why it wasn't normal.

She found humor in some of my bad habits and coping skills that I had learned well, but probably weren't the most desirable traits. She would laugh at me if she thought I was being ridiculous about something. She had ample opportunity, as I tended to take many things too personal. She was also the one that started taking me to the beauty salon to get my hair done. She would spend her own time coming to my room extra early, before school, to help me fix my hair until I learned to fix it myself.

"Tammy, girl, why are you crying? It looks good, girl. It looks *real* good." Ms. Span proclaimed as the beautician spun my chair around towards her away from the mirror.

"Ms. Span," I cried out, nearly jumping out of the chair, stripping the cape off. "Look," I said as I began caressing my hair that was no more on my neck or

122

shoulder line, "it's all gone. What am I going to do?" I asked her.

She grabbed me and pulled me in for a tight hug and said, "Please don't cry. You look real pretty. I promise. You're just not used to it. Come on now, let's get back home."

"But, Ms. Span, I can't go to school this way. I just started and people will laugh at me."

Trying to hold in a laugh herself, Ms. Span assured me no one would laugh at me. "It's not any different than when you pull it up in a pony-tail." She stated. She chuckled a little, but it was at my reaction and not my hair.

"Yes, it is," I insisted.

"You quit crying now. It will grow back. I'll come by and braid your hair for you, okay? Before school. I'll come by and braid it until it grows back out or you get used to it. You'll see, it will look so good and you won't have to worry about being laughed at."

I listened to her, but I couldn't imagine it. I was fifteen and my hair was all gone. I was so upset. When we returned to the cottage, Ms. Span braided my hair for me, to show me it could be done. I didn't know a person could braid that short of hair that tight, but it can be done. The other girls laughed at me making fun of the "white girl crying over her hair." I don't know that I ever cried about my hair before or since, but to this day, we still laugh about it.

Ms. Span also helped me to pick out clothes and makeup. In fact, one day she walked into my room saying, "Ooo girl! Tammy. We have got to do something with your makeup. Now don't be offended, but girl," she almost sang it to me, "you can not wear thirteen shades of eye shadow on one eyelid." Ms. Span was more into Whitney Houston than Cyndi Lauper, I determined. Hard to imagine that I thought it was okay to wear that many stripes of color on one eye, but it was the eighties and not so unheard of. After she toned down my application of shadows as well as thick lines of black liner on the tops and bottoms, I began seeing a new person emerging. No more when I looked in the mirror, was someone staring back at me hoping to be missed, but instead there was a young woman who was rather interesting and new.

My high school days, from second semester of tenth grade on, were nothing but pure fun. I attended Talladega High School, which for me seemed an enormous school, housing more kids than Chelsea Elementary and High School combined. Finding my way to the classes and trying to build new friendships came to me easier than I expected.

With less than two months under my belt at the school, Ms. Span approached me about cheerleading. "Tammy, I heard that they're having cheerleader try-outs. Why don't you go to the clinic so that you can meet people?"

Ms. Span was always surprising me. I remember looking at her as if she were an alien. Did she know who she was talking to? I hated cheerleaders, all except for Tiffany, of course. To me they were all uppities and I couldn't fathom being affiliated with them. Then as soon as I had the thought, I realized she was right. I had gotten to know several of them in class. They were friends of Katherine's, a classmate outside of the Home that I had really hit it off with. Here I was, new in a school, didn't know very many people, hadn't tried anything out of my

A Teacher's Prayer

comfort zone yet, and had been there two months. I said I was going to start over. Everything about me would be new, so what could it hurt? I wasn't going to make it anyway. I was in tenth grade, never cheered or desired to in my life, so I should simply do it to meet people. What a great idea. With that, I went out. This is when I realized that if I set my sights on a goal I would push myself no matter how relevant it was to me, because I couldn't do something half way.

I went through camp, met a lot of nice and funny people, and then we had try-outs. Who knew that cheering was really hard work? Who would have thought that it involved running for what seemed like forever up and down stairs in a gymnasium that circled to form a coliseum in the middle of the school? Or jumping repetitively by pushing on the back of a chair? Then there was tumbling, yelling, clapping, and continuously moving for two hours a day that week. I went through with it, even though I didn't want to, and it was a humbling experience as I realized the girls didn't just get out there and jump around to be cute, but were very athletic and worked hard to be on the squads. In addition to running laps, flipping and jumping, they stretched their bodies beyond normal limits, pushing themselves to perfection in a way I hadn't yet encountered. The team had to be unified in their cheers so everyone had to work hard to accomplish that. I went through the week, had a blast, but don't recall necessarily befriending anyone in particular. Maybe I was shyer than I gave myself credit for or maybe I was focused. I know it still didn't matter to me whether or not I made it, but for whatever reason, to me it did matter that I did my

125

best. As a result, I found myself pushing to be the best I could at something I didn't care a thing about.

On the day of postings, Ms. Span made me go look. I didn't want to because I knew it was pointless, but when she set her mind on something you couldn't change it, only do it. So, we went. Walking up to the glass door, she quickly took over, not worrying about whether or not I was standing beside her. She went up and with her finger, began scanning the document!

"Tammy! You did it! Come here, girl! You did it!" she yelled, acting as giddy as if she had just found out that she had been the one who had made it.

I had made it! How was that possible? I thought with my heart un-expectantly racing. I had actually made the cheerleading team! It was the JV team, not the Varsity, but I had made it. All of a sudden those jumps that I'd been learning for the past week were bubbling over inside of me, or should I say bouncing around on the outside. Ms. Span was just as happy as I was. I can't imagine the sight we must have been. While it was great for the moment, it would bring a heap of trouble to me. You can earn the team with the judges, but you cannot discount the team members and whether or not they accept you as one of them.

I was going into eleventh grade and all eleventh graders made the Varsity team but me and by making JV I knocked one of the tenth graders out. That did not settle well within the overall group. Cheerleaders have their little pack that they grow up cheering with throughout their school years and not only did I knock out one of the pack but I knocked out a sister of one the other cheerleaders. They had always cheered together, but apparently not that year, thanks to me. It was a rough start to the season, with a little resentment on the team except for a few of the girls. Mostly those on Varsity who I knew from class or church youth group and a couple on our squad warmed up to me quickly. Later that summer a slot opened on the squad so the younger sister who was runner up was provided the opportunity to cheer with us. These girls were all amazing. I cherish some very dear friends to this day, although we do not get to keep in touch very often.

When both Varsity and JV squads were together, I could hang a little with Varsity; but this was rare because we had separate practices and games. I don't know when things turned around for the better. It may have been after the slumber parties, when their mothers required them to invite the "whole JV squad" and they actually took the time to get to know me. It may have been the wear down of time which allowed them to finally accept me. Or I might have been graced with the presence of the sister making it—believe me when I say she deserved to be on the squad too—she was a very accomplished cheerleader. Whatever the reason, before the school year started, we had all become close friends. I am thankful for that today, because they were great for me. They also helped me to instill a different level of confidence that I had not known before. I believe after they got to know me they were rooting for my life to turn around as much as I was.

Between cheerleading and Ms. Span, I had no choice but to start believing in myself. Ms. Span had style and she was teaching me that. I remember not long after my Home days, I was speaking at a church. There I explained what it meant to that little, poor girl to get to wear a fifty dollar outfit. Was it necessary to spend that much money on a pair of jeans? Not really, but if spending that much money would give me a little confidence to walk into a public high school, feeling like the girl next door instead of a Home Kid, then the money was well spent. At some point, I began envisioning being able to grow up and dress as nicely as Ms. Span. Ms. Span wasn't just about appearances though. She was well-educated and you knew it when you spoke to her. In so many different ways, I looked up to her. My only connection to her was the fact that she was my social worker, but she was the kind of woman I wanted to become. I think Ms. Span knew a good foundation to starting my confidence was to teach me to look at myself in the mirror. Not to think highly of myself, but to respect myself and present myself in such a way. Maybe appearance is a girl thing, but it is important.

Ms. Span also pushed me to take advantage of opportunities at school. She had tackled my self esteem at the basic building blocks, but now, that foundation had to be built upon, and I guess she figured what better next step than school. She pushed, and I allowed her to, because I wanted more out of life. She had shown me that. I was busy adjusting to my new Home life and all the while, worrying about it being taken away. Therefore, not long after being at the Home, I decided it was time to take my mother to court and get custody of myself. The state appointed an attorney for me. The first time I met him was at the courthouse the day of the hearing. Never having been in a courthouse before, I found the long, mahogany benches lining the empty halls peaceful and assuring. There was a sense of respect within that building, similar to that of a library. If people spoke, it was very softly and not to be overheard by others, at least they spoke that way in the hallway. The ceilings were high above, dressed with crown molding, and the floors were that of a waxed-wood effect. Sitting in the hall with my attorney, Phillip, I patiently waited. We probably had conversations that revolved around reassurance, but mostly he was giving me advice on what to expect. Sitting there, I found myself nervous, but not about me. Instead I was scared that Mom would break out in tears before going on a rampage. She always told me as a child that no one would ever take me away. And even though I was stronger now, I was still worried that at any minute I would want to go running back home. I believed I had a choice; I just didn't know if I could withstand the pressure.

Walking into the courtroom, with my lawyer, I found the atmosphere like a movie, or at least a dream. What exactly was I doing there? I was introduced to the judge and she very patiently listened to me explain why I shouldn't have to go back home to my mother. She asked questions of me only when she needed more information; otherwise she directed most of the conversation to my attorney. This experience was far harder than walking out the door that night the few months prior.

I didn't want to hurt Mom, and as I spoke to the judge, telling her the details, things finally started sinking in. I could hear the words come out of my mouth about what happened to this teenage girl, even the little girl she once was, and I knew it wasn't okay. It was hard though because I didn't want to get my mother into trouble. The lawyer had informed me I would have to reveal the history of abuse in as much detail as possible. I knew I had no control over the judge's decision on what to do with the information that would be disclosed, but I did know I loved my mom very much and that I wanted the judge to know that too. No matter what, my mother didn't deserve to be treated badly. I made sure the judge heard me say that as well as know that she couldn't completely help all of the things that had occurred.

I told the judge all of it: about her boyfriends and what they did to me and about how important it was to ensure I never had to go back to where I came from; I also told the judge that my mom never hurt me and she was never around (at least not in the same room) when the incidents occurred. She was usually asleep or at a neighbor's. I wanted that judge to know that my mother was a good woman who had taught me right from wrong in the way I treated people, but that she couldn't keep me safe. I pled for the judge not to punish my mom, just to grant me the opportunity to have a say over my own life. To this day, I am as confident as I was then, that the judge listened to me.

I have faint memories of the judge tearing up, not while I told my stories, but when I told about how much my mother and I loved each other. I have tried to imagine what she must have said to my mother when she came in to meet with her. Did she get on to her, criticizing her tolerance of such men in our home? Did she lecture her about the precious gift and responsibility of having children? I can't be for sure and I have never asked Mom. No charges were pressed against my mother and for that I am thankful. I am thankful that judge knew that my life could be better than that which I had lived in and took away the fear of ever being forced to return. I never did

130

see Mom that day, which may have been by the design of the lawyer and social worker, or maybe even the judge. The judge did explain to me that my mother was accountable to my safety and my life before wishing me well. Phillip and I left the chamber and I would later find out that I won the custody suit.

Acts 3: 6 (NKJV)
Then Peter said, "Silver and gold I do not have,
but what I do have I give you.   In the name of Jesus
Christ of Nazareth,
rise up and walk."

Chapter 13 - Jordan Cottage

The Presbyterian Home for Children became my permanent residence. The grounds were set up quite a bit like a college campus. The cottages were age-specific and my initial residence there, Jordan Cottage, was the one allotted for teenage girls. It housed numerous bedrooms, a parlor, a kitchen, a huge den connected to a dining room, and a large multi-stall shower/bath on each end of the hall. Of course with seniority came the bedroom of your choice. It was a status symbol which indicated who ruled the roost. As girls got older and moved on to Johnson Cottage or even went back home, that would free up the larger rooms. Eventually I got my pick. My favorite room was on the west end of the cottage and located near the door. I was always coming and going, so it was a very convenient location for me. Plus, I pretty much got along with everyone and would get to speak with them as they entered and exited the door.

At the Home, Ms. Joni (the kids called her Ms. J.) was my first houseparent in Jordan Cottage. I found her incredible. She was young and full of creative ideas and Ms. J. possessed a tremendous heart for the ministry of the Children's Home. We all thought of her as a very 'cool' adult and mentor. The truth is, she just had a way with girls like us, carrying emotional baggage heavier than what was normally found. She knew how to let us be a little off the wall, yet expected us to know when to stop. Some nights all the girls in her cottage would end up in her room and pile up on the little sofa, or crowd in on the floor, just to watch television with her. We really enjoyed spending time there and she seemed to mutually relish the company. The houseparents had schedules that would allow them to work a few days on then a few days off, and when she was off we would count the days until she would return.

Ms. J. knew how to deal with troubled teenage girls and she had a house full; black and white, rich kids and poor, but she loved us all equally. The only time she treated us differently is when our actions warranted it. My little posse, or group of friends that I hung out with, really respected her in a way that not many other houseparents received. I think it was because Ms. J. did not reprimand us for everything we did wrong by raising her voice or belittling us, as most of us were used to in our previous home. Instead, she listened, allowed us to have our episodes and then go cool off. She would wait for us, until the point we realized we were out of line and then we, not her, would walk right back to apologize. Her firm and patient approach had a calming affect on all of us. This was a characteristic of many of the houseparents, but Ms. J. was exceptional at it.

Ms. J. was always concerned about how well we took care of ourselves, and used to worry about my sun-tanning habits. Behind our cottage was an old steel counter that came out of the kitchen, much like the counters you would find in a commercial kitchen, which we would call an Alabama tanning bed. I would slather on a thick layer of baby oil, pour peroxide over my hair and then lay out on top of the counter to soak in as many sun rays as possible. Ms. J. was never very fond of tanning, probably because she had somewhat pale-colored skin, and maybe too because she knew it may not have been good for us. Yet back in the 80s we were all about tanning, and because of it, she allowed us to turn up the radio inside, open the windows and lay out beneath the sun. She always chose her battles well and this was one she didn't feel a need to fight.

She only drew the line with us when we crossed over by being disrespectful or hurting one another. She lived up to her motherly role for all of us girls: cooking, doing laundry, cleaning, making us clean, and she was also very crafty. One year for Christmas Ms. J. made each of us a beautiful photo album. Mine was a lovely print of yellow with white flowers and had my name embroidered on the front of it. I still pull it out to this day and look at. I didn't understand at the time just how talented she was.

Ms. J also instilled in me the art of collecting Kool-Aid points. One day at the cottage, not long after I arrived, she called me into the kitchen.

"Tammy, come here for a moment please."

"Yes, ma'am?" I said, as I turned from the hall into the kitchen.

"Do you like Kool-Aid?" Ms. J. asked while standing there mixing a packet of red Kool-Aid with a cup of sugar and some water.

"Sure," I replied.

"Grab some cups," she suggested then poured us both a glass.

"Did you know that you can get free things if you save the packets?" Ms. J. asked me.

"Really? Free?" I inquired.

"Yeah," she said with a little chuckle, sensing I liked the word *free.*

"Like, what kind of things and how do you do that?" I asked, so excited that I didn't give her time to respond to the first question before demanding the answer to them both.

"Well, do you see the points right here?" she asked, pointing to the back, bottom right corner of the packet. "I just cut them out, save them up and then mail them in. They have a number you can call to request a catalog."

"Huh. Neat." Surprised by what I had just learned, Ms. J. had my attention. My whole life I had been drinking Kool-Aid—at least when we could afford it—but never knew those little numbers on the back meant something could be gotten for free. I think this is when my learning addiction kicked in. I realized, regardless of how important this particular moment seemed, that there was so much out there that I was clueless about. Who knew you could mail in for free, nice things like slip-n-slides, games, and so on? I sure didn't. I am happy to say that since my time at the Home and learning about saving points, I have saved my fair share of Kool-Aid points and now am the proud owner of a Kool-Aid man pitcher and four matching cups. That red pitcher and its cups have happily resided in my home for the last eighteen years, and are still very useful.

As stated, Ms. Joni put up with a lot of stress from us girls, but we knew she genuinely loved us and I thank God she was there to help me transition. Words could never do justice to the woman who gave me my first example of a good motherly role. Not to knock my own mother, because again, she was one hundred percent of the mother she could be. Ms. J. gave me a different example, and one that I model my own role after today. I had the pleasure to send her a letter and get back in touch with her, thanking her for the difference she made in my life.

A Teacher's Prayer

Too many times, people who choose to reach out to children in need, go unnoticed and unappreciated. They don't always get to know exactly what an impact they had. I know that many of my friends today that used to live at the Home hold Ms. J. in the highest regards because she was one of a kind.

Ms. J. and I recently met up again at a PHC reunion along with a couple of the other girls who lived there at the same time. We laughed, walking the halls of Jordan Cottage, remembering how much trouble we caused her. The same kind of laugh my kids and I have today when we reminisce about their younger days and the silly things they tried to pull. It was reassuring, rehashing the good ole days with my Home family. The family bond was real and still alive in all of us. On that day, Ms. J. shared with me that she remembered everything about each child that came to live there under her care. Of course, I had a question for her.

"What do you remember about me?"

"Tammy, I remember, you were a very closed off, quiet and scared young lady."

"Really?" I asked her, laughing, not even beginning to imagine that I was ever shy or closed off.

What a testament to the Home and to Ms. J. I was closed off when I got there. I absolutely did not recall that until she said it; I had to stop and think. She was right. I was desolate, isolated and scared until I realized life was wide open and I could fully embrace it if I chose. I took a chance because I had precious people pushing me and believing in me. They provided me a safe outlet to grow in and I had a blast. It is because those people loved me through my darkest days that helped me begin to build my future.

Today Ms. J. is a seamstress shop supervisor for Hollywood movies and I understand she still uses the "Huth Syrum." I am going to leave that up to interpretation for the readers, but I will say, she never has had to raise her voice or reprimand, she simply speaks and you know to get it together. For the record, I love to see Joni's name roll on the credits and wonder if the people working with her today know what a wonderful, amazing human being they have met? I wonder how many more lives she has touched and I pray to God that she knows how much she has touched mine. I am grateful for her friendship that continues today. Her impact on my life could never be justified by words.

I can't finish the story about Ms. J. and me without telling one more tidbit. Ms. J. informed me that one of the things she never figured out was how I fit into my group of friends that I made at the Home. Normally that group did not let people in. I still laugh thinking about it, because I have no clue. Just never thought about it that way. I was closed off and I went to group counseling with some of those girls. Let's just say they were determined to break me down and make me talk. Not an easy thing for someone who has never been to counseling before and especially for someone who doesn't want to tell anything private, that is nobody's business.

I remember one young lady, in particular, one of the meanest of our group, getting in my face, all the while pointing a finger so close at me that I was sure she would poke me.

A Teacher's Prayer

"You think you've got crap (but she said a different word), you've got no more crap than we do. Get over yourself."

I still laugh. She was serious and she was mad at me for staying shut off from everyone. I couldn't possibly sit there and not open up. No telling how miserable they would've made my life if they thought that I thought I was better than they were. I didn't, by any means, but they didn't know that. I think once they 'convinced me' to open up, they had a sense of pride and responsibility to me. I am so thankful for their friendships because without them, I might not have ever dealt with my "stuff." I love you girls and you know who you are and that I mean it!

We were a tight-knit group of young ladies that stories are written about, and there are countless numbers lying on the shelf that I cannot possibly get to. One of my favorite that often comes up whenever we are together is about an occurrence that happened right before I moved out of Jordan Cottage. There were many occasions that we snuck out of the cottage at night. Usually it was to go meet guys. While I never did anything worse than kiss one or drink a little, it was still the point of daring to do something that was forbidden.

One day, one of my friends came up to me at school, to inform me we would be sneaking out that night. There were four of us girls who were really tight at the time and supposedly this would be our biggest moment yet, as we were going to steal the cottage minivan keys from our houseparent's room and go for a ride. Or at least that was the hype at school. We were full of hype. I never really knew when it would play out, up until the last minute. They didn't include me in the planning, only the executing.

That day after school I went back to the cottage and got started on my homework. It was after supper and I was sitting at a desk in my room with a dim lamp adding extra lighting to my books when one of the girls walked in and spoke to me.

"Tammy, she stole the keys and we are going to sneak out tonight. She really did it. She got the keys."

"Really? Okay," I responded, completely caught up in my studies and not being easily distracted, for I had a test the next day.

"So, aren't you going to come?"

I laughed at her in disbelief and said, "No, I've got homework to finish."

"Okay then. You sleep in, but I'm going."

There was no way they stole the keys out of that room. No possible way. Plus, they didn't know how to drive. What in the world would they do with the keys if they stole them? Go sit in the van and smoke a cigarette? Turn up the radio, just to prove they could steal the keys. That sounded exactly like something they would do, but I had to focus on my homework so didn't give it another thought. That night I went to bed, not thinking another thing about it. The next morning, bright and early I awoke to someone shaking me.

"Tammy, wake up. They ran away! Get up—they ran away!"

Still somewhat unconscious, I began to arouse and realized one of the girls was sitting on my bed with her arm in a sling—the same girl that invited me to go with them.

A Teacher's Prayer

"What?" I asked, dazed and still groggy. Looking in disbelief, I quickly sat up.

"What happened?" I asked again.

"They ran away." She called them by name and explained to me what had taken place. That they did indeed steel the keys and went to one of the girl's homes. As they were leaving, it appears a tree just jumped out behind them and rammed itself right into the back of the minivan. The young lady sitting on my bed was only there because she had to be taken to the hospital. At least our friends were responsible in that way. The crash threw her into the floor board, causing her to break her arm and tearing up the car.

She now had my full attention and I was incredibly alert, sitting up in bed, beginning to worry. She rambled on, explaining that Ms. Leslie was on the phone with them, assuring them that she was safe. As she continued, her storytelling grew to concern, as she had explained that after they dropped her off, they ran away because they didn't want to go to jail. At the mention of jail, I jumped out of bed and headed in a bee line to Ms. Leslie, with tears in my eyes, ready to beg on their behalf. Unfortunately I couldn't find Ms. Leslie, as she was behind closed doors. So I waited.

Ms. Leslie eventually convinced them to return to the Home, and we all went back to normal. This, of course, included their getting grounded — which really was normal in itself. Maybe this was my first sign of how valuable getting a good education could be at keeping you out of trouble.

Not long after this incident, I entered the eleventh grade and got to move into Johnson Cottage, also known as Independent Living. While staying there I obtained my learner's permit, then my driver's license, and became more involved at school, developing some lasting friendships. The independence that came with living there was definitely a part of helping me grow into a young woman. We learned to budget our allowance and entertainment monies. We took turns preparing menus and cooking dinner. We washed our own clothes and had chores for specific duties in the cottage; all of which we had to complete or get docked for. My houseparents were wonderful and my time there flew by fast.

Days at the Home revolved around studying, playing and hanging out. It consisted of growing confidence, finding security and knowledge. I had the pleasure to get to know many of the kids at the Home during the short span I was there and am so thankful for all of their friendships to this day.

The summer before my senior year would be a life-altering one for me. I had found my oldest brother, Jimmy, again and the Home agreed to let me fly to Arizona to stay with him for a week or so. He was a truck driver and was so happy to be having me come to visit. Overall, we had a great time that summer. We tubed the Colorado River, rode Jeeps off-road, and took a road trip in his rig to Nevada, passing over Hoover Dam. Unfortunately, my brother was still tripping on drugs. Since I was unaware of that, I discovered that I would never have the relationship with him that I had hoped I would. And that was disappointing.

A Teacher's Prayer

Psalms 139: 17-18
How precious also are Your thoughts to me, o God!
How great is the sum of them!
If I should count them, they would be more
in number than the sand;
When I awake, I am still with You.

CHAPTER 14 – Talladega High School

My eleventh grade year was phenomenal. My grades continued to improve and yet again I befriended several teachers who pushed me and challenged me in more ways than just studies. They encouraged me to run for offices in clubs and to take on outside extracurricular activities. I believe the change in my life, my ambitions, and my vision of what my future could be came not just from the Home and the counseling, but also my friends and my teachers. I also believe that a large part was an ability to be aware of and take a hold of whatever opportunity was provided. I know beyond a shadow of a doubt that all of those silent, unknown prayers that were lifted up to heaven on my behalf played the most important role in that change.

One man in particular was Mr. C. He was one of the most incredible influences that drove and pushed me outside of my comfort zone in school. I remember sitting down in his Economics & Government class and being taken aback by his introduction. He started out his roll calling in such a unique way, "Miss Crosby, Mr. Jones... Miss Mentzer..." one by one he addressed each of us by last name and then introduced himself by his last name. He then went on to tell us that we were getting older and what we would take from his class would be up to us. That we will have so many influences come and go and that by studying history and understanding the importance of our rights and freedoms in economics and government, not only would we shape our own future but that of generations to come. He was different from most teachers in that he was able to assign, instill, and expect a

143

level of maturity from his class; so much so that he commanded a captive audience every day. Our class would not only include lectures, but debates and opportunities for real world experiences with voting and courtrooms outside of his class. The reason I mention him, is because he would become as important of a drive in my life to believe in myself and succeed as Ms. Span had already been. God used Mr. C. to become a personal friend; someone I could trust, but also learn from his wisdom. He was the first man that I had trusted in a long time to give any credibility to and to listen for any length of time. This was yet another wall being broken down. My trust was going beyond just the maternal figures in my life.

This year I became more involved with the youth group at our church. The youth were led by Mrs. Becky and Mr. Morris, who was also the Director over Social Services at the Home and Ms. Span's boss. Only a couple of the kids from the Home actually attended the youth group at First Presbyterian, but we usually averaged around ten kids in attendance. I had been invited by Katherine, who would become one of my dearest friends at the high school. Our youth group set a foundation for me unlike my other church experiences. With this group, I was free to be a teenager. To grow and study at a slower pace; to apply what I learned in an instructional manner, as I did with my studies at school. No longer was it taking every single word and reading it literally, but it became about learning from history and making it a life application. The Bible became a story, not to seek out answers as to why things were happening to me, but to

144

drive me through instruction how to live out my life, how to become a better person.

Mr. Morris and I would grow closer because of his participation with the youth group. He was the first fatherly role, since my dad's death, that I remember and I will always be grateful for his sincerity in wanting my life to be something more.

My eleventh grade year centered around discovering great new friends at the high school. How blessed I am to look back and realize how very many friends I made at Talladega, from all different walks of life. Each one impacting me by their kindness, humor, academia enlightenment, and even sometimes their strangeness. An oddity about that year was just this, because prior in my life, I had never sought out friends at school before, nor did I desire to. In addition to increasing my friend circle, my grades were improving steadily as I began taking advanced classes and really aiming for college preparatory schedules. I left my eleventh grade year knowing that my life really had started over and I wanted to continue on the new path I had found.

In twelfth grade, I moved from Advanced into Advanced Placement courses, with grades and progress continuing to impress the school, the Home and even myself. I was making mostly A's with some B's. Science was always my weakness. Advanced Placement English was probably my favorite because we studied a lot of college literature and I could really get caught up in aspirations and dreams. It was what my life had become about.

This year, I also made the Varsity Cheerleading team and I loved every moment. I want to say again, those girls work hard, and anyone who says differently needs to try it on for size. In addition to cheerleading, I had the opportunity to join a high school sorority, Double Nine, which at the time was the only one at our school. It afforded me the opportunity to make another set of friends, attend socials and take in a few extra dances. I can't even put into words the impact all of these girls made in my life. Whether they are aware or not, I watched each of them. I got to choose the characteristics I liked and didn't like and in a way replicate those within my own ideals. I was conscientiously deciding how I could grow and change and learning did not just root in the book sense, but in what I liked about their behaviors and habits. They seemed very confident and smart and tended to know what they wanted out of life. I was at a point in my experience where I knew I wanted to do more than just quit high school and go work at McDonald's, so I needed to find out what other possibilities lay ahead. At our sleepovers I would get to see beautiful homes and understand that an education enabled their parents to be doctors, lawyers, nurses and educators. I got to see first hand that they were loved and comfortable in their environment. They also influenced me in other ways, some not so good; but again, this was my choice at the time. Of course I went to parties and probably did some things I shouldn't have, but this was me being a teen.

I know in writing my story that throughout, especially in the hard times, I acknowledge God and my dependency on His Word and faith. It was still very alive and a part of me during this time as well. Yet, instead of seeking refuge in Him for myself, I began finding Him living out loud amongst the people: the friends like those in my youth group, on my squad, in my classrooms, the teachers at the high school and counselors at the Home. Even my friends who did drugs and drank represented kindness and acceptance and believed in me as one of them. This is when I learned it is very important not to seclude people or judge them because they do not share the exact same values as you. Of course I had my temptations too. I was not perfect and I would be lying if I said I didn't have fun, but every step I took in the world was not only an experience to enjoy but was held accountable by Him at all times. I made some worldly decisions being a teenager and enjoying so many freedoms of high school, but I also dealt with growth and accountability, sometimes painfully. My conscience was now speaking to me in a voice I had never known before, holding me accountable for my ways.

The beginning of my senior year was very exciting. Our teachers called it senior fever and the students called it Senioritis. But true Senioritis didn't hit until after Christmas break. The senior year of high school is so unlike others. People were becoming more mature. The assumption is that when you become a senior you are one step closer to being a full-fledged adult. It's amazing how that mentality actually seeps into teenagers and begins to overrule hormones and thoughts of others. It's the year when there are subtle but noticeable changes in personalities. Stress related to performance and preparation seeped into our lives. No more was it just about being at the greatest party, but there became a sense of urgency to focus on entrance exams and aptitude test results. Before our senior year, the only ones who really seemed to care about their test results were the really smart kids that already knew their grades before they came.

Predictably, there were a lot of breakups. For some reason, during that senior year, the person that they had been dating all through school, or just steady since eleventh grade, was all of a sudden not mature enough or directed enough. Maybe before it didn't matter; they were just dating and having a good time. It wasn't hard to state that you had a relationship because you were in high school and you still had the rest of your life ahead of you. However, it was during that senior year or the summer leading up to it that our eyes began to open. These quickly maturing young adults began to realize that these weren't the persons with whom they wanted to spend the rest of their lives. I was right there with everyone else, dating and breaking up, taking tests, focusing on exams. The sky was the limit. I'd become a normal-looking, normal-acting kid. I went to church youth, but I must admit, it became more of a social gathering than a spiritual building time. However, I had a fantastic youth director who continued to show me the same unconditional love that my school bus driver did so long before.

Looking back, I know God found other ways to keep me accountable while living up the world. He grounded me amongst some dear ladies and friends — older adults in our church — by interesting me in the church choir and hand-bells. I by no means had natural talent, but the beauty of the praise time I spent with Him, focusing on the meaning of the words of worship and sounds were an altogether different growth in Him at that time in my life. Through my teachers and adult friends from church, their stories would only enrich my walk with

A Teacher's Prayer

Christ as I learned to balance my worldly ways with my spiritual walk. It will take time, however, and for their examples I would be forever grateful. Please understand I am not okaying my worldly walk, just pointing out that it was normal for me as a teenager. If people had pointed fingers at me, passed judgment and condemned me instead of loving me, it might have pushed me farther from God instead of pulling me closer to Him. Those ladies at the church knew I wasn't perfect in my behavior, as did Ms. Becky and Mr. Morris, but they kept loving me and inviting me to come back time and again. When telling my story, I always look back at the realization that I was fifteen when I left home and started my life over. It is never too late to reach a child, so I hope we never give up on our youth. We need to set expectations, but we also need to love them for who they are. Not pass judgment, but show them by example how we are called to live. One will turn away quicker from judgment than from acceptance and love. Look at the difference in my learning when comparing the behaviors towards me by the students at Chelsea versus the behaviors of the students at Talladega. So I know my peers had just as significant of an impact as the adults on the way my life would be enhanced.

Philippians 4:8 (NKJV)
Finally, brethren, whatever things are true, whatever things are noble, whatever things are just, whatever things are pure, whatever things are lovely, whatever things are of good report, if there is any virtue and if there is anything praiseworthy- meditate on these things.
The things which you learned and received and heard and saw

A Teacher's Prayer

in me, these do, and the God of peace
will be with you.

Chapter 15 – The Power of Prayer

The first time I ever saw the ocean came about on a youth trip one summer prior to my senior year. I was so overwhelmed with the vast open water which one could see for endless miles. I'd never seen anything like it. The road leading to it was less than appealing to the eye with the typical tourist buildup that overruns many coastal areas. Everywhere I looked was shop after shop of tourist attractions, condominiums and hotels stacked one right on top of the other and very small parking places lining the main road. I was not all that excited at first because it wasn't the look I had become attracted to. The look a girl from beautiful Alabama, with all of its greenery, rolling hills and trees was used to seeing. That is, until all of the clutter was removed and I gazed beyond the hustle and caught my very first glimpse of the ocean.

I had known it was there, but it exceeded any expectation I could've ever envisioned. So vast, so wide open—and it extended farther than my eyes could see. I was overwhelmed by the sheer magnificence of it. It's hard to imagine the comprehension and awe that set in the first time I laid eyes upon it, but I still remember it. I still get those butterflies in my stomach and the tingling when I reminisce. The ocean is so picturesque from the outside looking on. I remember definitively thinking, "Wow, God created this for us and I have never seen it before."

One night while there, I sat on the balcony patio taking in all the sounds and senses that come during a visit to the beach. The other girls were getting on their PJs, talking and giggling about the guys they had talked to that day. I simply sat out on the patio listening to the rushing waves crashing against the sand and rocks. I couldn't see except for other lights from rooms that stretched down the beach or an occasional glimmer as a wave fell perfectly to reflect a little light my way. It didn't matter though, because my soul was quite overcome with peace as I listened to those waves splash and birds scream their night sounds. There were no crickets or frogs to be heard, and as I sat there, I began to sense that I knew exactly how that ocean must feel. To be so large and seem so grand yet it was constantly rushing up onto the sand against the rocks only to be pulled right back out into the vast path it had come in on. It was then, on that night, that I wrote the following:

> *I feel as a wave crashing against the rocks,*
> *My motions and purposes stronger than my will.*
> *I look up to the sky and see the freeness found there,*
> *Yet how is it I am destined to smash?*
>
> *No I'm not allowed to roam the world where I wish;*
> *I'm only destined to follow a course.*
> *People think that I'm stronger than I am;*
> *If they only saw the helplessness and weaknesses I felt.*

There was a poetry contest at school my senior year, and I submitted the poem from that summer. Talladega High School was a 6A school, so a very large one. Everyone who had English class, from ninth up through twelfth, had to participate for a letter grade. This poem became the poem that I submitted and actually won second place with. That last semester of my senior year, The Presbyterian Home published the poem in the Home newsletter, a regular publication for all of its donors to keep updated on the events for the children as well as to print names of memorials and honoraries. It also included a section of trips, a heartfelt story about a child and announcements of birthdays and school accomplishments.

That semester, the newsletter contained my senior portrait and beside it a special insert of my poem and my accomplishments in school. Shortly after this mail out took place, I received a card regarding my announcement. I had received numerous cards for my birthdays and for Christmas, but never received one from a stranger for no apparent reason. It was then that I would learn the true power of prayer. God usually does show us answers to prayers; they're just not always obvious at the time. As I opened it and began to read, I became very intent on each word.

> *Dearest Tammy,*
> *I saw your picture in the newsletter and was so proud to see that you are doing well in school. I have thought of you and Sammy over the years and wondered how you were doing because I knew that you had left home…*

I was stunned because the person wrote to me as if they knew me. Sam's name wasn't in the newsletter; he did not live at the Presbyterian Home for Children. He still lived at home with Mom. Who in the world could it possibly be? I continued reading.

> *…I am not sure if you remember me, but this is Mrs. Lokey and I taught you in second grade…*

A Teacher's Prayer

I couldn't believe it. My second grade teacher? Writing to me? I was perplexed trying to figure out how in the world she found me. The rest of the letter read as follows:

> *I will try to come to the Home for Visitor's Day as I would like to see you again. Congratulations again on your graduation and your poem. I am so proud of you.*
> *With Love,*
> *Mrs. Lokey.*

I couldn't believe my eyes. What in the world were the chances of my second grade teacher recognizing me? It wasn't like I looked the same by any means, but then again, not just anyone in Alabama had the name Tammy Mentzer.

I was so thrilled over the note that I must have told everyone about it. My houseparents, my social worker, my friends, my current teachers and even my Mom. Ms. Span immediately encouraged me to write her back to thank her for the note and express how I was looking forward to seeing her. I decided to make it a personal note and let her know how much I remembered about her too; after all it would show my gratitude. The problem was my memory being of that standing in the lunch line, kissing a boy and getting in trouble for it. While I don't remember what all I had written to her, this was her final response back to me.

Dear Tammy,

It was so good to hear from you. Again let me say how proud of you I am for doing so well in school but most of all because you want to do something with your life!

A Teacher's Prayer

I don't remember the incident of your kissing Brian in the lunch line-I hope I didn't make too much of a "to-do" about it....I know you'll be busy but it would be nice to hear from you occasionally-If I can help at anytime let me know....

"Go gettum, Tammy."

> *Happy 18th Birthday,*
> *Love,*
> *Mrs. Lokey.*

Yes, Mrs. Lokey was true to her word. She showed up at Visitor's Day in April and we did get to meet. It was amazing how similar she looked to me — almost exactly the way I remembered her. I would've recognized her anywhere, but there was one thing different. She wasn't this stern teacher that I was somewhat intimidated by as a second grader; but instead she was one whom I held in great awe for caring so deeply about me that she would remember me over all of those years. When we met that day, she shared with me that she'd been praying for me through all of the years, since I had been in her class. At the time, I didn't make the connection, but it amazes me now to think of the story. If she received the newsletter then she was supporting that home financially with her offerings. There is no telling how long she'd been doing it or whatever made her start doing it. The fact is that she had been praying for me all of those years. I don't think it sheer coincidence that I eventually came to live at the Presbyterian Home for Children in Talladega, Alabama. I thank God that Mrs. Lokey has had the opportunity to see a sincere and selfless prayer come true.

A Teacher's Prayer

John 15: 17 -18 (NKJV)
*If you abide in me, and My words abide in you,
You will ask what you desire, and it shall be done for you.
By this My Father is glorified that you bear much fruit;
So you will be My disciples.*

CHAPTER 16 – High School Graduation

High School graduation was a night all its own. My graduation night was so incredible that there aren't enough words to explain it: a time when teenagers are dressed in their Sunday best, running to and fro, receiving kisses from moms and aunts, as well as huge hugs or slaps on the back from proud fathers and grandpas. With all of the noise, someone would have expected there to be a concert going on, but there is no way to fathom a concert that would join this many different generations with laughter.

It was my very own special moment to remember, something I had worked hard for. There was so much laughter and gabbing as we forced our ways in towards the mirror. Talking to ourselves and each other in the mirror was something that we girls had done on numerous occasions before, but this time it was very different. There was a lot of giggling and goal sharing and of course, still conversations of parties afterwards.

I stood there in amazement wondering how in the world I'd come so far in such a short time. It was funny, the girls were either standing around talking about the guys or they were finalizing plans for parties that were to follow this major event. I, on the other hand, was absorbing every precious moment: the laughter, the teasing, the adjustments and the dreaming as I prepared to march toward that stage and receive my diploma. Time was literally passing in slow motion and I took in every second around me — the full experience.

This wasn't just another teenage milestone to accomplish; this was a major feat for me, being the very first in my family to graduate from high school. I stood there, staring in the mirror at the young lady I had become. Spiral-perm, brown hair and makeup dazzled to a tee, no one from back home would've recognized me. I adjusted my cap, making sure not to mess up my bangs and then took a deep breath, being immensely grateful for this special opportunity. It really felt quite surreal.

Standing there, gazing into the mirror, I can still remember my red, oversized robe hanging on me like royalty — or at least that was how I felt on that night. While I stood higher than many of the girls at my school, reaching 5'7", I had a 26" waist and when you looked at me, you could see it in my face and my bones. It wasn't that I was malnourished; I had actually ingested more food in the past two and a half years than I probably had in any given time of my whole life preceding the day I moved out of my house.

As the finishing touches were being applied to each of us girls (by this I mean the teachers coming by and smashing our doo's to sit the caps flat on our heads), I knew that my moment was finally here.

This was it, the big night I had worked so hard for in the last two and a half years, I thought to myself, taking a deep breath, wanting to relish every second. Normally I would be searching the world over to be nearest to my friends, but tonight was something I wanted to take in and savor by myself, the gratification of the long, yet short, road behind me. Besides, we were in a procession line by alphabetical order to lead into the gymnasium and find our seats to await the calling of each graduate's name. It was the night I was proving that I could indeed be anything I wanted to be. And it was that thought that almost made me miss my cue. I had butterflies swarming in my stomach as I realized my name was next.

I only had one wish to make the day perfect. It was that my father could see me. Oh how I prayed to God that He would grant one wish to allow Daddy to look down on me from heaven on that particular day and be proud that his little girl made it, even without him here to cheer her on. On graduation night, the emotions that I experienced are difficult to describe. To have worked so hard in such a short time, to have had so much support from so many different people and yet not to have my family there to see me receive my reward. Joy and disappointment both began to settle. They *were* there though, I just didn't know it. I saw my mother and Sam after the ceremony, brought by my best friend, Jen, from childhood and her mom, Renate. Also present were all of the teachers who pushed me since I arrived in Talladega as well as all of the support staff from the Home in which I had resided the past two years.

The most unexplainable visitor was the one person I prayed for—my daddy to be watching over me. He wasn't literally present, and I could only cling to a hopeful prayer that somehow he had to know from up above. While praying for God to tell my dad, I heard my name called out. Stepping onto the stage, my hands sweating, I looked the principal straight in his eyes, knowing that I couldn't wipe that huge smile off of my face. I just wanted to jump up and hug him, but I simply took the paper while shaking his hand, telling him thank you; and then turned to head off the left side of the stage. My focus had turned to, *I did it,* and not tripping as I walked back to my seat. As I stepped down the third and final stair, I felt overwhelming warmth circumvent me, as if I were walking outside in a beautiful field on an early spring day and everything seemed perfect. My heart flushed with warmth and tears of joy drifted down my face. I knew my Daddy was with me and had just wrapped around me; and this feeling was more than I had ever hoped for or thought possible. I thanked God for that moment.

Isaiah 40:31 (NRSV)
Those who wait for the Lord shall renew their strength, they shall mount up with wings like eagles, they shall run and not be weary, they shall walk and not faint.

A Teacher's Prayer

Epilogue

The first in my family to graduate from both high school and college, I had big ambitions for my life. Graduating with an Advanced Diploma after turning my life around in approximately two and a half years, I had beaten the odds. I would also graduate from college years later with a BBA, concentration in Human Resources Management. Absolutely, I sit and realize many of times just how blessed I have been to be given the opportunity to start my life over and obtain an amazing family, a good education and a good job.

Not to end the book on my high school years alone, let me tell you about my family. With all of the education I have received, I must say I continue to grow and learn about the plans that God has for me. Family lifestyle has not come easy for me, especially when I was going through my workaholic stages.

Patrick and I met early in our first year at college and I am sure that was in God's plans.

Unfortunately, I was living a worldly life and my grades were not a focus—just enjoying the college social life and cheering. However, I would make some amazing friends who tried to keep me grounded and continued to discuss our relationship with God. I think this is one of the reasons I sought out a relationship with someone who had that part of his life together. One day, while crossing opposite sides of the lawn, he caught my eye. Approximately six feet tall, short, light brown hair and a well-dressed young man, I found him immensely attractive. It was one of those moments when you are just walking along and notice someone. I tapped my

161

roommate, who was walking with me, on her arm and said,

"Check him out."

She then raised her hand and yelled out, "Hey, Patrick!"

"What?" I asked of her. "You know him? Who is he? What do you know about him?"

She began telling me that he had gone to high school with some of our dorm buddies and after inquiring of him, I learned that he was a Christian and a very good person. The intrigue came more about not just his being attractive, but because I knew he was living the way I should've been. I wasn't sure if we would date or not, but I didn't mind finding out more about him. We didn't have classes together, but the campus was so small it wouldn't be that hard to learn the other important details.

As it turned out, Patrick had also noticed me on more than one occasion and had been inquiring as well. He was just shy. One day during our campus group picture, Patrick and I finally had the opportunity to meet. We started hanging out, going to lunch regularly, sitting on the tennis courts talking about classes and a little bit about our backgrounds; schools where we came from and the like. I had no clue that I was getting to know the one person that would help me overcome one of my biggest barriers in life and teach me how to really love a family, for the first time.

Patrick and I stayed friends from October through January, again hanging out on a regular basis, but we were only friends. Deep down, we both wanted to be more, but it took another dear friend, Kevin, to help make that happen. One day after returning from Christmas holidays and at the start of our second semester, Patrick asked me out on a date.

Being quite the gentlemen, he swept me off of my feet when upon arrival he opened his car door and a single red, rose lay in the seat. We went to dinner, a movie and then returned to the dorm.

We married in December of 1991 and while it has not been easy, it has been amazing. To have the opportunity to know someone who makes the world a better place just by being in it, then to get to love them and have them love you back is truly a remarkable gift. Patrick has taught me to believe in the values of a marriage and family and for this I am forever grateful.

We have two incredible children for whom I give thanks every time I see or think of them. Unfortunately for them, at times I can be overprotective, and at other times a little too mushy, like when they were younger and I was sitting at McDonalds allowing a tear to drop down my face because I knew my kids were safe and I knew to be thankful that I could afford to feed them.

Anthony is attending the University of Alabama, while his sister Lauren is enjoying High School. I have had some reality checks in the past twenty years that nothing, no matter how wonderful, is easy or perfect. I live every day with the reminder of my father being taken so young, so I try to live for every moment in appreciation of them in my life. I don't always show this, but I hope that for the most part I do. In marriage and family, we have had our struggles as almost all of us do, but continuously God has graced us with strength, compassion, forgiveness and perseverance.

A Teacher's Prayer

Anthony and Lauren are amazing blessings to our lives and they bring such joy to the both of us. Lauren worries her dad more now that she is approaching teenage years, but we wouldn't trade this for anything. The things which I am most proud of my children for are their personal relationships with God, the way they treat others, and their goals and aspirations within their own daily living, including school and church. But I know not to take these for granted. I do share them however, because these are some of the reasons for the immense amount of joy they bring to our lives.

Together our family has learned, and still continues, to place Christ first, family second, and careers or school third. This lesson has taken me far longer to learn than any of them. If I had to choose only one thing I would want my children to retain as the lesson they learned from me, it would be that in my own life, through experience, I have gained some innate wisdom that I know the Lord has plans for them: "...plans to prosper and not to harm..." We will walk on this earth and experience trials; He says that we will. But, in and through it all, He promises to be there with us. The most releasing scripture to which I have clung is that He chose me. This amazing Being who created everything and has ultimate power over life and death actually chose me and He chose them, and He chooses you, too!

In August of 2003, while speaking with a group of women about my testimony, two retired teachers approached me to thank me for sharing the story. I had just started writing this book two months before and had been praying hard for some direction on where it should go. I love young people and know that there are so many out there who don't know what it feels like to truly hear the words, "I love you!" or "I believe in you." I thought that was my message, *Make sure you reach out and never give up on a child.* It was while sharing this that I remembered Mrs. Lokey and what she had meant to my life as I began sharing the segment of receiving her card after the poem was published in the newsletter. The women seemed genuinely touched by the story and it was then that I realized how much love all teachers must have for children to do what they do for a profession.

While driving home following the speaking engagement, I began thanking God for all teachers who chose their careers to benefit the lives of children. I began to think of the role so many teachers had in my life, and in particular, the role of Mrs. Lokey. The possibility that her prayers helped guide me to the Presbyterian Home so many years after sitting in her class, was breathtaking. This is when, during yet another prayer, the title *"A Teacher's Prayer"* and the fact that Mrs. Lokey's faith should be the inspiration for telling my story came about.

When I got home, I asked my husband to go up into the attic and retrieve the hope chest which housed my memorabilia from high school and college. I was hoping, from the depths of my heart, that I had kept one of Mrs. Lokey's letters from years ago. Patrick, being used to, and a little frustrated with, my "gotta do it now" personality, agreed to go and find my hope chest. Of course he gave me a little bit of a hard time about not being willing to wait until daylight.

He descended the last stair and planted the big, grey chest at my feet in the middle of the living room floor. I opened it, joyously recalling the memories I had locked away.   Similar to the memories I had forgotten in any detail before writing this book. I found my high school scrap book and slowly flipped through the pages, taking one more glance at pictures of old friends and acquaintances that I had lost touch with over the years. Reading over newsletters and cards of "What I want to be when I grow up" from various students, trying to compare their wants to the outcomes when I was last updated. I finally got to a newsletter from the Home; it was the one which published my poem. Turning the page, I found an envelope from Mrs. Lokey and read each word aloud. I laugh today even thinking about it. It was the one of my memory of kissing a boy in the second grade lunch line, the same boy I couldn't recall while writing this story.

Quickly sitting down at my desk, I began to write Mrs. Lokey in an attempt to "keep in touch," and all I could do was hope to write something sincere and personal, without saying too much. I did so and mailed it to the same address on the outside of the envelope.

August 18, 2003

Dear Mrs. Lokey,
I am not sure if this letter will find you or how it will find you but I do send it with great thanksgiving for what you have meant to my life. I pray that it will find you and your family all doing well. I am working on writing a book and it will be titled (or at least I anticipate it to be), A Teacher's Prayer. It will be highlights of my life story with a spiritual emphasis but it will also be about the people who have made a difference in my life. I would like to include a brief part of our story. I hope that you will not mind, please let me

know...I just can't begin to tell you about all of the wonderful things life has shown me since living at the Presbyterian Home. I also can't begin to thank you enough for caring about me beyond the school setting. Teachers are such a wonderful and special gift to children and I am so glad that you allowed God to use you the way He chose to. I do pray that this letter finds you doing well and just wanted to let you know that I was thinking of you as I have so many times before. The difference is this time I am writing to you because I found a card you sent me for my 18th birthday and you asked me to keep in touch...at some point I forgot to do so and I wanted to try to catch up with you again. Please write if you can because I would love to stay in touch. If you do write, please tell me about your family. I will do the same in return-of course in more detail than I have here.

Sincerely and with love in Christ,
Tammy Mentzer Brown

I just hope that reading this little bit there is a realization that if we don't get out of our own little world and take time to look around us and reach out then we may miss out on a lot of good to come in both their lives and our own. Was it the faithful prayers of that second grade teacher which initiated the turn towards a better future in my life or was it the faithful prayers of that anonymous spiritual benefactor which led to my changes? Whoever and how ever many, I thank God every day for the people in my life. I do believe He gives us different people at different times in our lives to meet our needs and to lay out the plans He has prepared for us. The following is the response I received from her.

August 25, 2003

Dear Tammy,

Thank you so much for your sweet letter. It was such a wonderful surprise to hear from you. First of all let me say how elated I am to know that you are a Christian. God is so good and He's so great. He has blessed me in too many ways to count and forever students like you are one of the reasons God led me to be a teacher. I'd feel honored if I was remembered in any small way in your book. Hope you pursue these accomplishments until it's complete...

Tammy, I am so proud of you! You have accomplished so much in your short life. I had a chuckle when I read your comment about your family (You sound exactly like me). You said your pride and joy were your husband and children....Thank you for making your life count for Him in such a wonderful, positive way. Remember me to your children, Anthony and Lauren and to your hubby as well.

With Christ's Love,
Mrs. Lokey

So how do I end this story? The perfect way would be closure about the teacher who inspired the title and brought some semblance to the enormous effects of prayers. Therefore I did not want to publish so quickly without trying to find Mrs. Lokey one more time. Over the years, I have sent Christmas cards, but lately have not heard back. As I set out to Google her location, I became somewhat discouraged as it was seemingly hopeless to find her yet again. My husband reminded me that if I thought of her as a grandmotherly figure in second grade, I would be lucky to find her at all now. So, I decided to go ahead and publish based on our correspondence and got out the letters we had written to each other back in 2003.

I had not given up completely on finding Mrs. Lokey. I decided to go about it a different way. I Googled Chelsea Elementary School and dialed what I thought was the school I had attended. After explaining my purpose, stating that I was getting ready to publish a book and really needed help finding my second grade teacher from the seventies, I was told that I had actually reached the Intermediate School. They, of course, could be of no help but referred me to the Elementary School. It was then that I learned Chelsea was no longer K-12, so they referred me to the Board of Education and finally, coincidentally enough, I reached her niece who worked there. She put me in touch with Mrs. Lokey's daughter, who, once I reached, explained to me that they had found the copy of my manuscript which I had sent to Mrs. Lokey, while cleaning out their mother's things from her home. She then updated me on her mother, who was currently in an Assisted Living Home and doing very well. Her daughter stated that she would love a visit from me and while she may not remember me, she does remember teaching and would be excited to meet a former student. We talked for a while as I told her about my story and the impact her mother had on me and then I asked her if she knew how Mrs. Lokey had received the newsletter that year. She stated that her mother had sent memorials to the Home as loved ones or friends passed, that she was fond of the children's home.

I did go to meet Mrs. Lokey recently, along with my husband and two children. She was so energetic, full of life and moving faster than I was. We enjoyed a pleasant lunch with her and her daughter, catching up on everything. What blessed me most of all was having the opportunity to tell her what a blessing she had been to me and how grateful I was for her relationship with God. She hugged me so big and told me many times that I would never know how much it meant to her for me to remember her and be there to share that with her. I would learn a little more about Mrs. Lokey that day. How she lost her father in a work accident at age three. I learned about how proud she was of her daughter and son too, just like I am. And that she loved gardening and even showed me the beautiful limbs of a potted rose bush she was able to tend to, compliments from her son. The biggest thing I took from her that day was just how very much she loved being a teacher. She might have asked me a few questions repetitively while we visited, but her memory of her love for teaching was never a question, nor the blessing it brought to her to have a former student remember her for it.

So I end this book, knowing that my life has been blessed because of the people whose paths I crossed, even if only briefly. My hope and prayer is that the witness of this testimony clearly displays that we all have choices to make in our lives. This book is not to preach or push my religious beliefs onto others. It is to share a story about a mighty God that we can serve. If I have one mother (or father) that reads this and questions if they can/should be a better parent; or one (preferably thousands of children) who say "If she went through that and did something with her life then I can too;" and/or one teacher keeps praying for the desperate child in his or her classroom he or she cannot seem to reach, and through it all know that God is in control, then this book has a purpose and the things I went through in my life have a purpose and therefore made the journey worth the walk.

Revelation 12:11 states, "For they overcame him by the blood of the Lamb and the word of their testimony." Your testimony might be something you too become burdened to share. Dear friends, your testimony may also be the way you live your life! I have some absolutely amazingly beautiful friends who tell me, "Tammy, I never had an a-ha moment or tragedy other than not getting a job I wanted, or whatever." I say "You are the testimony. You are the friends who listened and prayed with me when I couldn't, or when I didn't even know I needed it. You were the friends who offered me a place to stay or lunch money. You were the one who smiled at me today. You were the ones who took me in and accepted me for who I was." Dear reader, remember, your testimony is always the way you live your life. You are God's witness here on earth in your actions and your words. Please do not miss the opportunity to serve God in all that you do. If the words come in thoughts, remember that prayer is powerful too!

A Teacher's Prayer

John 15:16-17 (NKJV)

*You did not choose Me, but I chose you and appointed you that
you should go and bear fruit,
and that your fruit should remain, that whatever you ask the
Father in My name He may give you. These things I command
you that you love one another.*

A Teacher's Prayer

Frances Lokey, born October 20, 1921 still resides in Birmingham, Alabama today. The seventh of eight children, which included only one sister, she is the only surviving sibling. Mrs. Lokey's parents immigrated to the USA in the early 1900's from Russia and Poland. They met through a Polish newspaper and came to Birmingham and married. What seemed to be a story-book beginning, meeting that special someone and moving to a country of opportunity, would soon turn tragic as Mrs. Lokey at age three, would lose her father, giving up his own life in the mines, while trying to save others who were trapped. Through her mother's will and perseverance, Mrs. Lokey would grow up a strong young woman and complete college at Auburn University after WWII. She stayed with her mother until the boys came home from the war. It was at Auburn that she married her husband, in September 1947 and within the next six years gave birth to their two children. They lived on a farm, and in 1953 their home was struck by a tornado. Their safety assured as their dad protected them all under a mattress, only afterwards to find the entire house completely gone, except the floor they were on. Mrs. Lokey began teaching in 1954 and she retired sometime in the 1980s. Unfortunately, Mrs. Lokey would experience loss again, as her own husband passed in a work accident on December 16, 1967. Both children were off to school and their lives, as they say it, and Mrs. Lokey would pour her life into her teaching the "precious children" she got to love. She was an active church member and a very generous woman.

Mrs. Lokey touched many lives like mine, but ironically enough, her contributions to the Presbyterian Home for Children and her prayers to God, would set up a different kind of path to turn my life around. It would be in 2011 when preparing to publish my memoir I would discover two unique coincidences, one suspected, but not confirmed until then and the other not even imagined: 1) that the teacher who wrote me saying she had been praying for me since second grade had been sponsoring the Children's Home in which I inadvertently would come to reside and turn my life around; and 2) that maybe fate even had a deeper connection in that we both lost our fathers at an early age in life. May you come to believe in the power of prayer and service as witnessed by the many testimonials in this book!

Man Crushed To Death in Work Accident

Sam Mentzer, 37, of 824 Fourth street NW was pronounced dead on arrival at Mercy hospital Thursday afternoon following an industrial accident at Iowa Steel and Iron Works, Inc., 400 Twelfth avenue SE.

A spokesman for the company, Larry Cratty, said a 20,000 pound counter weight to a large crane "shifted" and pinned Mentzer between the weight and a flask. The flask, filled with sand and metal, is used to make castings.

Mentzer was employed in the foundry department. He had worked for the company for 10 years.

Cratty said police investigators were at the scene following the 5:50 p.m. accident. He said the weight crushed Mentzer's back.

* * *

Sam F. Mentzer, 37, formerly of Anamosa, had been a Cedar Rapids resident the last four years. He was born Aug. 11, 1939, in Coggon and was married to Diane Hope Wolfe. He was a member of the Cedar Rapids Cactus club and the Teamsters union, and he attended Edgewood Baptist church.

Surviving in addition to his wife are a son, Sam, jr., at home; a daughter, Tammy Kay, at home, and two sisters, Mrs. Barbara Stetler, Oxford Junction, and Mrs. Myrtle Floyd, Anamosa.

Services are pending at Cedar Memorial funeral home, where friends may call after noon Monday. Burial: Garden of Eternal Love section of Cedar Memorial cemetery.

May, 1990

Tammy Mentzer is a senior and an "A" student at Talladega High School. She is a varsity cheerleader and a member of the girls' high school softball team. Tammy won second place in the high school division of the poetry competition of the Alabama Penmanship Contest sponsored by the Talladega Arts Council. After graduation, Tammy plans to attend Walker Junior College.

Destined

I feel as a wave, crashing against a rock.
My motions and purposes stronger than my will.
I look up to the sky and see the freeness found there.
Yet, how is it I am destined to smash?

No, I'm not allowed to roam the world where I wish.
I am only destined to follow a course.
People think I am stronger than I am.
If they only saw the helplessness and weaknesses
I felt.

Tammy Mentzer

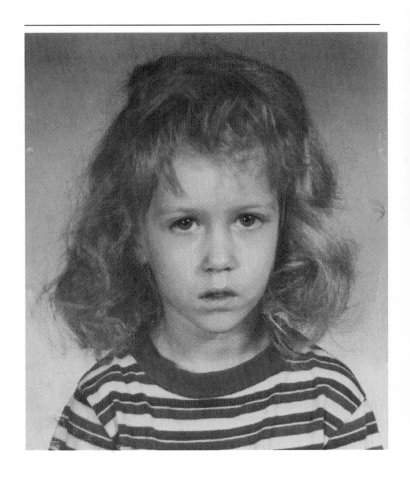

Tammy as a Child

Tammy's High School Graduation